ORNAMENTATION
AND
ILLUSTRATIONS FROM
THE
KELMSCOTT
CHAUCER

Published in Canada by General Publishing
Company, Ltd., 30 Lesmill Road, Don Mills,
Toronto, Ontario.
Published in the United Kingdom by Constable
and Company, Ltd., 10 Orange Street, London
WC 2.

William Morris—Ornamentation and Illustra-
tions from the Kelmscott Chaucer, first published by Dover Publications, Inc., in 1973, contains all the illustrations and a selection of text
pages and decorations from *The Works of Geof-*
frey Chaucer as published by William Morris's
Kelmscott Press in 1896. A new Introduction by
Fridolf Johnson and a Publisher's Note have been
added in the present edition.

International Standard Book Number: 0-486-22970-X
Library of Congress Catalog Card Number: 73-80560

Manufactured in the United States of America
Dover Publications, Inc.
180 Varick Street
New York, N.Y. 10014

WILLIAM MORRIS

☙

ORNAMENTATION
AND
ILLUSTRATIONS FROM
THE
KELMSCOTT
CHAUCER

With an Introduction by
FRIDOLF JOHNSON

DOVER PUBLICATIONS, INC., NEW YORK

PUBLISHER'S NOTE

In the present volume, 100 pages have been reproduced from the original *Kelmscott Chaucer*, one of the supreme achievements in the history of book making. These pages contain all 87 of the woodcut illustrations after designs by Burne-Jones and all of Morris's large borders and decorated initial words. A supplementary section gives examples of all the ornamented initial letters which Morris designed for the *Kelmscott Chaucer*.

The pages are reproduced at 72 percent of their original size. Their original sequence has been altered to retain their left-hand or right-hand position, but all double-page spreads have been retained. The title of the work or section from which each page has been taken appears at the bottom of the page. Words which originally appeared in red are shown in gray.

Because the text of Chaucer's works is readily available, we have not reproduced complete stories or passages. However, in order to acquaint the reader with the basic layout of the book and the appearance of the less decorated pages, three typical double-page spreads have been included (see our pp. 102-107).

The publisher wishes to thank the Library of Congress for generously lending a copy of the original edition. We are especially grateful to Mr. Frederick R. Goff, Chief of the Rare Book Division, for making this loan possible.

Published in Canada by General Publishing Company, Ltd., 30 Lesmill Road, Don Mills, Toronto, Ontario.

Published in the United Kingdom by Constable and Company, Ltd., 10 Orange Street, London WC 2.

William Morris—Ornamentation and Illustrations from the Kelmscott Chaucer, first published by Dover Publications, Inc., in 1973, contains all the illustrations and a selection of text p⌣ and decorations from *The Works of Geoffrey ⌣ .aucer* as published by William Morris's Kelmscott Press in 1896. A new Introduction by Fridolf Johnson and a Publisher's Note have been added in the present edition.

International Standard Book Number: 0-486-22970-X
Library of Congress Catalog Card Number: 73-80560

Manufactured in the United States of America
Dover Publications, Inc.
180 Varick Street
New York, N.Y. 10014

INTRODUCTION

William Morris (1834-1896) was indubitably the most influential figure in the history of the decorative arts during the last hundred years. And the *Kelmscott Chaucer*, from which the following plates have been made, was most certainly Morris's crowning achievement. A full appreciation of its splendor and a true comprehension of its magnitude require some knowledge of the man who created it.

William Morris's total contribution to society is difficult to assess because his extraordinary genius touched on many aspects of art and human affairs. He was a prolific writer, speaker and polemicist as well as an artist. A man of means, he gave unstintingly of his time and substance fighting for what he conceived to be man's inalienable right to happiness and dignity. The exploitation of the poor, the squalor of their existence, the stifling dullness of middle-class life—all by-products of the Industrial Revolution—were to him intolerable. The tastelessness of manufactured goods, he felt, were evils that could be done away with by a return to the medieval ideal of honest, individual craftsmanship; to produce what one needed with one's own hands was the ultimate good. So far as he was concerned, genuine civilization ended when the Renaissance began.

He was a leader in several societies, and carried on a vigorous campaign against misguided "restorations" of ancient buildings. One of his last public appearances was at the first meeting of the Society for Checking the Abuses of Public Advertising. He travelled extensively in Europe; he went to Iceland, steeping himself in Icelandic sagas. He was a social animal who conducted a voluminous correspondence.

And finally, during the last half dozen years of his busy life, Morris revolutionized the art of printing; or rather he lifted contemporary printing from a routine trade into a high art. His influence upon the printing arts was profound and pervasive; even in America, the decorative printing of the nineties and the first few decades of the twentieth century cannot be properly appraised without frequent reference to William Morris and his Kelmscott Press. The works of the Kelmscott Press will stand forever as monuments in the history of printing, and the name of William Morris, it may be, will stand second in rank to that of Gutenberg.

William Morris was born March 24, 1834, at Elm House, Walthamstow, then a prosperous, large village since become a dingy suburb of greater London. His father was moderately wealthy, and as the family expanded they moved into an impressive Palladian mansion which included a private brewery, bakery and buttery. As a child, William was delicate, and he naturally turned to books for companionship; he was said to have been reading Scott's novels at the age of four. Epping Forest was just outside his back door, and as he grew stronger he spent more and more time exploring the countryside, acquiring the intimate knowledge of botanical forms that he later put to good use in his decorative designs. There were plenty of ancient buildings and churches to explore; his youthful imagination was fired by these and Scott's stories of brave knights and fair maidens, and by the time he went to Oxford he was a confirmed medievalist.

William had decided to become a High Church clergyman, but he was bitterly disappointed with Oxford; he thought it was stuffy and reactionary. It was there that he formed one of the warmest friendships of his life. Edward Burne-Jones was also headed for the ministry, but the two young men became lost in long discussions about matters that had little to do with the church. Gradually they realized that art and literature were their true vocations; they made brass rubbings, took up wood engraving, modelling and illumination; they discovered Ruskin and read Chaucer aloud.

William inherited a monthly income of 900 pounds when he came of age. He used part of the money to found a literary review, *The Oxford and Cambridge Magazine*, and began to write prose romances for it. The magazine lasted through 12 monthly issues. Then Morris decided to become an architect and entered an architect's office in London. There he made another lasting friendship; this time with Philip Webb, an employee assigned to show him the ropes.

Here again he felt he had made a mistake, finding the routine chores of an architect's assistant tedious and unfulfilling. His life at this time was brightened by the arrival of his friend Burne-Jones, who had come to study art under the great Pre-Raphaelite painter and poet Dante Gabriel Rossetti. Morris made frequent visits to the studio and Rossetti soon convinced him that painting was the supreme art. In 1856 Morris announced that he would become a painter, and he and Burne-Jones took a house at 17 Red Lion Square.

Morris and Burne-Jones thoroughly enjoyed life in their bachelor diggings. Not being able to find the truly Gothic furnishings they desired, Morris designed a number of pieces to be built by a local carpenter. The large, bulky wardrobe and other items were decorated by Burne-Jones with scenes from medieval legends. Brimming with ideas and ideals, they dreamed impossible dreams that later, in part at least, miraculously came true. There was much horseplay and noise at all hours. Morris early exhibited a violent temper that he never quite brought under control; their landlady was alternately terrified and scandalized at their pranks.

Morris applied himself strenuously to painting, trying to give concrete form to his romantic visions of medieval pageantry. But he was never satisfied with what he did, and left most of his work unfinished. He also fell in love with his model, Jane Burden. She was a stableman's daughter, the ideal type of Pre-Raphaelite beauty: tall and slender, with a long neck, dark, dreamy eyes, heavy black eyebrows and a huge mane of black hair. There is a story that one day Morris turned over a study he was making of her and scrawled on the back, "I cannot paint you, but I love you." Rossetti was also in love with her, but Jane's practical instincts prompted her to marry the prosperous Morris, and the marriage took place in 1859. The only surviving oil painting by Morris is of Jane Burden as "La Belle Iseult" (1858), now in the Tate Gallery, London.

Jane posed frequently for Rossetti as well. A Victorian sense of propriety has drawn a veil over Morris's relations with his wife and Rossetti, but enough is now known about the love affair between Jane and Rossetti to account for what was once unexplainable. In this light, some of Rossetti's sonnets in *The House of Life* take on a darker meaning, and the unbearable impasse would explain Morris's compulsion for over-extending himself in all directions.

Morris discovered his true bent when he built a home for himself and his bride. Philip Webb was the architect, and it has been written about as a turning point in architectural history. Christened Red House, it caused considerable comment because it had been planned from the inside out instead of cramping the rooms behind a stiff facade. That the construction was allowed to show here and there in the interior was another novelty.

Morris spent several years furnishing the house in the Gothic style he loved. It was full of stained glass panels, tapestries, embroideries and huge Gothic furniture, all specially made. Morris not only designed nearly every piece, but had a hand in executing many of them, meanwhile making exhaustive studies of materials and techniques. While the work was in progress, there were regular gatherings of like-minded friends at Red House. Inevitably, they agreed to establish an art decorators' studio. Thus the firm of Morris, Marshall, Faulkner & Company was founded in 1861. There were seven partners, including Morris, Webb, Burne-Jones, Rossetti and Madox Brown. Later the firm came into Morris's control and was known as Morris & Company. It was finally liquidated in 1940, 44 years after Morris's death.

The firm expanded rapidly, setting up showrooms and a kiln for firing stained glass and tiles, and gradually assembled a corps of craftsmen. Later they set up a dyeing and weaving plant at Merton Abbey, on the Thames.

Morris took charge of the designing, and his output was phenomenal. He made over 500 designs and patterns for stock wallpapers, carpets, textiles and tapestries, besides innumerable individual designs for embroidery, textiles and stained glass. He supervised the production of more than 500 stained-glass windows, for which he had supplied another 200 or more figures and patterns. He busied himself with craft experiments, and seemed especially to enjoy the manual work of dyeing and weaving. With the exception of some collaboration with Webb on complete decorative schemes, and helping Burne-Jones with the drawings for some early stained-glass windows, Morris's principal design work was for surface decoration. He was a master pattern maker and produced patterns with astonishing ease.

In between, he continued to write, shifting easily from designing to writing and back again, picking up where he left off without hesitation. His literary production kept pace with his designing, and verse flowed freely from his fertile mind. On one occasion he began working at four in the morning and did not stop until he had turned out 750 lines. Altogether he published seven lengthy volumes of original poetry, four of prose romances, six of prose and verse translations and two of lectures. The Memorial Edition of his works, published in 1912, ran to 24 chunky volumes. His place in literature is secure, and rests upon two or three superlative books and poems. As for the rest, it requires some perseverance to read them through now. In spite of some striking images, the very ease with which he composed produced a flood of flaccid sentences that for most modern readers soon leads to ennui.

William Morris had always been interested in books; he owned a great number of them. Oddly enough, he handled them carelessly, and was perfectly capable of leaving a volume out in the rain. From time to time he had acquired some particularly fine illuminated manuscripts and incunabula. He himself made numerous manuscript books of his own, writing the text in a variety of scripts and decorating the pages with illuminated initials and borders. Most of these are extant in private and public collections. The writing is in a beautifully controlled hand, and the free-flowing decorations are delicate, the colors clear and soft.

That Morris should eventually turn his hand to the production of fine books was inevitable. He had already shown considerable interest in the niceties of typography, and took a small part in the design of some volumes of his narrative poems. As early as 1866, Morris had begun a scheme for an illustrated folio edition of *The Earthly Paradise*, to be printed at the Chiswick Press. Burne-Jones had made more than 100 designs for the illustrations, 35 of which had been cut on wood by Morris himself, and the rest by four other engravers. Specimen pages were set up in Caslon type. The project was abandoned finally because of technical defects in both typography and woodcuts of the trial proofs made by Chiswick.

The genesis of the Kelmscott Press dates from November 15, 1888, after Morris had attended a lecture by his friend and neighbor Emery Walker on the connection between medieval illuminated manuscripts and the incunabula modelled after them. As the two walked home that evening, Morris expressed a desire to design and have cast a new font of type. The following month he was already at work on the project.

Instead of choosing a Gothic model for his first type, as might have been expected, Morris based his design upon the superb roman type of Nicolas Jenson, the fifteenth-century Venetian printer. It was an excellent choice. Working from enlarged photographs of Jenson's type, Morris made large-scale verisons of his own design, and then had them reduced photographically to the size in which the new type was to be cut. Each letter was painstakingly studied and revised; steel punches were then made, and these too were carefully revised. The complete set of punches was finished in December, 1890, and type-founding of his new face, called Golden, began.

Morris designed two other types: Troy and Chaucer. The Troy type, which he preferred to the other two, shows the influence of the early types of Peter Schoeffer of Mainz, Gunther Zainer of Augsburg and Anthony Koburger of Nuremberg. It is a strong, rounded, blackletter, somewhat darker in mass than the Golden, but easily readable. It was named after the first Kelmscott book in which it was used: *The Recuyell of the Historyes of Troye*, issued in November, 1892. The Chaucer type is actually but a smaller version of the Troy type, being Pica instead of Great Primer (before the point system came into use, the various sizes of types were designated by name). The Chaucer was first used in the same book for the list of chapters and the glossary.

Jenson's magnificent type had been disregarded up until then, but Morris's version of it caught on, and in America an imitation of the Golden type was founded and called Kelmscott. There was a great revival of interest in Jenson's type, and other versions quickly followed: Venetian became a generic term in the trade for all types of this character. Morris's Troy type was also imitated in numerous variations, some of them inept.

Initially, Morris had planned to set up his own typesetting shop and have the books printed elsewhere. But it soon became obvious that nothing short of complete control of all the elements of book production could satisfy him. He therefore installed a hand press in a rented cottage near his Hammersmith residence and looked for workmen. He shopped around for the finest inks and commissioned Joseph Batchelor to supply hand-made paper with a specially designed watermark.

Morris's first book was to have been Caxton's translation of *The Golden Legend* of Voragine, for which he named his first type. But the first batch of paper received from the mill was not of a suitable size; the text was too long, and Morris was impatient to produce his first book. He therefore chose a shorter composition of his own, *The Story of the Glittering Plain*, and the first trial page was pulled January 31, 1891. The presswork was finished on April 4, and the book was published May 8. (It should be mentioned here that Morris never served his apprenticeship as a printer; actual production was left to his workmen, but under his careful scrutiny.)

Morris thought of his press as a private venture, conducted for his own satisfaction and at his own expense. Twenty copies only of the *Glittering Plain* were to have been printed for distribution among his personal friends. But news of the work leaked out and Morris was persuaded, against his inclination, to print an additional amount for sale. Two hundred copies on paper, besides six on vellum, were printed, with a single woodcut border and twenty different decorative initials.

The book created a sensation among printers and collectors, and was followed later that year by the second Kelmscott book, *Poems by the Way*, in an edition of 300 copies. This was similar to the first book in format, but with the addition of red ink. Meanwhile, work on *The Golden Legend* had already been started, but because of its length, it became the seventh book to be issued from the press. By that time, Morris had pretty well established a style for all the books to come, with woodcut borders and initials designed by him, and illustrations by Burne-Jones, Walter Crane and C. M. Gere. Altogether, there were 53 titles, in editions totaling 18,234 volumes, produced from 1891 to when the press was closed down in 1898, two years after Morris's death.

The Kelmscott decorations are, of course, the features most commonly associated with the press. The magnificent presswork, the fine paper and the general "feel" of the books are pleasures limited to those privileged to possess or examine them. Morris was continually designing decorations, initials, borders and ornaments for the books. He himself said, "It was only natural that I, a decorator by profession, should attempt to ornament my books suitably; about this matter I will only say that I have always tried to keep in mind the necessity for making my decorations a part of the page of type."

As some initials were discarded, Morris designed new ones, gradually making the foliage larger and the backgrounds lighter. Altogether he designed no less than 384 initials of various sizes; of the letter *T* alone there are at least 34 varieties. These, together with the borders, title pages, inscriptions, frames and printers' marks, total 664 separate designs by Morris, drawn and engraved within the space of seven years.

The majority of the blocks were engraved on wood by William Harcourt Hooper, a consummate old craftsman who enthusiastically emerged from his retirement to participate in the work of the press. Printing was done from the original blocks, except where duplications, especially of initials, necessitated the making of electrotypes. The electrotypes have since been destroyed and the blocks deposited in the British Museum, not to be used before 1998, and then only under rigid restrictions.

In reviewing the work of Morris, one naturally wonders how so much could be done by one man in a comparatively short lifetime. Philip Henderson, in his excellent biography of Morris, writes: "it should always be remembered that work was for him a pleasurable exercise of his energies; it actually refreshed him; and that his idea of recreation . . . was simply a change of occupation. Most of his writing was a form of half-wakeful dreaming and, together with his designing, was done, as Yeats observed, 'with an unheard of ease and simplicity.' A great part of his designing was, in fact, a glorified form of doodling, with which he wove his cocoon against the world. Intellectual effort, therefore, scarcely entered into it; it was almost as natural as breathing."

It should also be noted that Morris was never at a loss for decorative motifs; his mind was full of them, gleaned from his youthful rambles in Epping Forest and from hours spent poring over medieval herbals.

H. Halliday Sparling, in his book on William Morris and the Kelmscott Press, quotes a description of Morris's working method written by W. R. Lethaby:

> I have watched Mr. Morris designing the black and white borders for his books. He would have two saucers, one of India ink, the other of Chinese white. Then, making the slightest indications of the main stems of the patterns he had in mind, with pencil, he would begin at once his finished final ornament by covering a length of ground with one brush and painting the pattern with the other. If a part did not satisfy him, the other brush covered it up again, and again he set to put in his finished ornament. This procedure opens up another idea of his, that a given piece of work was best done once for all, and that all making of elaborate cartoons, and then accurately copying into a clear finished drawing, was a mistake. There was not only a loss of vitality which would come by the interposition of more or less mechanical work, but a drawing would not come right a second time, and would always to his eye bear the impress of a copy instead of a thing self-springing under his hand. It is difficult to realize the extent to which he felt this, but . . . he seemed to have the idea that a harmonious piece of work needed to be the result of one flow of mind; like a bronze casting in which all kinds of patching and adding are blemishes. . . . The actual drawing with the brush was an agreeable sensation to him; the

forms were led along and bent over and rounded at the edges with definite pleasure; they were *stroked* into place, as it were, with a sensation like that of smoothing a cat . . . thus he kept alive every part of his work by growing the pattern, as I have said, bit by bit, solving the turns and twists as he came to them. It was to express this sensuous pleasure that he used to say that all good designing was felt in the stomach.

The Kelmscott books, appearing during the general ferment of the Arts and Crafts Movement, naturally encouraged the establishment of other private presses, and trade publishers followed the trend by paying more attention to the formats of their books. And there was a great awakening of interest in printed bibelots and little magazines, in which literary content was only too often secondary to the style in which they were printed.

Morris's example of using woodcut decorations exclusively was not followed to any great extent. Making drawings in imitation of woodcuts and having them photoengraved was simpler and less troublesome. The new process of photoengraving stimulated the use of work frankly produced by the pen, and hand-drawn letters for display lines and initial letters became a handy substitute for typography. For better or for worse, the white-on-black tone of the woodcut gradually shaded into the lighter complexion of the drawn black line on the white background. The greater freedom of pen-and-ink rendering drove a wedge between artist and typographer , and the perfect harmony which once existed between type and the hand-cut block was soon lost sight of.

There is scarcely a printer or typographic designer achieving prominence during the first part of our century who was not for a time under the spell of William Morris. The early work of such masters as D. B. Updike, John Henry Nash, Frederic Goudy, Will Bradley and Bruce Rogers shows clearly the influence of Morris. Sooner or later, each had absorbed the lesson and departed in his own way from the Morris pattern while retaining his ideals of meticulous craftsmanship. Bruce Rogers, more independent from the beginning, only hinted at his debt to Morris, saying, "for in those days we all liked heavier and cruder types than our reconsideration of the matter now leads some of us to prefer. It may be that my eye reacted earlier than most from the types made popular in the nineties by the so-called revival of printing."

Will Bradley, perhaps the most engaging printer and designer of this period, cut some blocks that are almost pure Kelmscott. He drew frequently with the pen, also, combining heavily decorated borders and Beardsleyesque illustrations having large areas of solid black or repeat patterns. He was attracted to the quaint printing, the crude woodcuts and the Caslon types of the Colonial period; his uninhibited adaptations of these elements created a style that was unique. Bradley was enormously gifted and versatile, and he lived and worked to a ripe old age, much loved and admired by designers of the older generations.

The late T. M. Cleland, early in his distinguished career, spent so much time gazing spellbound at a copy of the *Kelmscott Chaucer* displayed in the window of Scribner's bookshop on Fifth Avenue in New York, that an employee invited him inside to take a closer look. He was shown many more Kelmscott books and other fine items, and promptly decided to have a press of his own. The young man set up a shop, the Cornhill Press, in Boston, but lack of funds and adequate support forced him to give it up after a year. He had printed several small books on this press; they are collectors' items now. At least half of them are clearly patterned after Morris's work. After a few failures at the woodcut, he switched to pen and ink, perfecting the firm, clean lines and impeccable taste that later made him famous.

The fashion for decorative borders initiated by Morris was long kept alive in large measure by Cleland, whose pen-drawn ornaments, brilliantly evocative of French eighteenth-century decoration, were high spots in the advertising and editorial art of the twenties and thirties. This vogue for fine borders and ornaments brought frequent and lucrative commissions to such gifted designers as O. W. Jaquish, Clarence P. Hornung, Walter Dorwin Teague, George F. Trenholm, Carlton D. Ellinger, Bertram Goodhue and Paul Ressinger. Much of this fine work, ephemeral in nature, is now lost to sight, buried under the effluvia of recent decades.

In a Kelmscott book, the decorative borders and large initials are reserved for the opening spread or beginning of a new chapter. The remainder of the pages are quite simple, consisting of text, compactly arranged, perhaps a small initial or two, surrounded by ample, carefully considered white margins. Unhappily, the frequent reproduction of only opening pages gave rise to the notion that every single page was heavily decorated. This misconception spawned a plethora of overwhelmingly decorated Kelmscott imitations, books stupefying in their monotonous repetition, page after page, of ill-conceived "designs." Such monsters, in the guise of "deluxe" editions, gift books, memorial volumes and school yearbooks mercifully do not appear as often as they once did.

It would probably be kinder not to mention those who, without taste or understanding, plagiarized the Kelmscott style. They have been deservedly forgotten; all except, perhaps, Elbert Hubbard and his Roycroft Press. A retired businessman, Hubbard visited Morris in 1892. Inspired by what he saw there—or rather electrified into action—Hubbard set up shop in East Aurora, N. Y., and soon had a good thing going. He not only had a printshop, but a congeries of pseudo-medieval craft shops, a smithy and a furniture factory; also an inn for the accommodation of visitors who came from far and wide to gaze at his fake picturesqueness and listen to his cultural doubletalk. At one time he had over 500 employees. His journal, *The Philistine*, largely written by himself, had a circulation of nearly a quarter of a million. The Roycroft books, atrocious specimens of spurious craftsmanship, had a ready sale at the time. When Morris's daughter May travelled to Buffalo, N. Y. to speak to the Women's Club there, she indignantly refused an invitation to visit Roycroft, exclaiming, "I most certainly will not go to Aurora, nor do I have any desire to see that obnoxious imitator of my dear father!"

Just the same, Hubbard did much to stir up general interest in cultural matters; the public taste being what it was at the time, perhaps he was no more than it deserved.

THE KELMSCOTT CHAUCER

We now come to the specific subject of this book: the Kelmscott edition of *The Works of Geoffrey Chaucer* and its decorations. The *Chaucer* is easily the most ambitious and widely celebrated production of the Kelmscott Press. It is impressive for bulk alone: a folio of 556 pages printed in black and red, with 87 woodcuts after designs by Burne-Jones; a double-page title, 14 large borders, 18 borders or frames for the pictures, 26 large initial words and innumerable ornamented initial letters large and small, all drawn by William Morris and cut on wood. The title page, one of the finest Morris had ever drawn, took two weeks for him to do.

Morris also designed the bindings. The ordinary edition was bound in half-holland; a specially designed binding was executed in white pigskin over oak boards and with silver clasps. The design was stamped by hand, a work which occupied a man six days for each volume. The paper was specially made, entirely of linen, and it has a watermark of a perch with a spray in his mouth; this was the third of Morris's watermarks, the others being the daisy and the apple. The book was heavily oversubscribed and Morris added another 100 copies to the edition. Besides the 425 copies on paper at £ 20 each, there were 13 copies printed on vellum, of which only 8 were for sale at £ 120 each.

All the decorations were cut by Hooper. It was also Hooper who so admirably engraved the illustrations by Burne-Jones. Burne-Jones had made a great number of illustrations for Kelmscott books. But Burne-Jones had little understanding of woodcut technique and it had been necessary for someone else to translate his drawings into designs suitable for cutting. His designs were nearly all in pencil and were redrawn in ink by R. Catterson-Smith, and in a few cases by C. Fairfax Murray; they were then revised by the artist and transferred to the wood by photography. It was a painfully long process, and Morris was discouraged by the long delays caused, especially in the production of the *Chaucer*— Hooper spent an entire week on the cutting of each of the 87 pictures for this book. But Morris had chosen his illustrator wisely, and the work of Burne-Jones perfectly reflects the Kelmscott concept.

Morris had begun thinking about the *Chaucer* as early as 1892; the following year he was already at work designing the title page and other decorations. Because of its length, the text was set in the Chaucer type, in double columns for compactness. For the headings, Morris used the larger Troy type. Actual work on the *Chaucer* had started on August 1, 1892. It was finished May 8, 1896, and publication date set for June 26.

On the second day of June, 1896, the first two completed copies of the *Chaucer* were delivered to Morris from the binder; one was meant for Burne-Jones, the other for himself. He was sick and worn out, relieved that the great work was finished at last. Exactly four months later, on October 3, he was dead at age 62. William Morris was buried in the little churchyard at Kelmscott, where visitors may see the simple stone designed by his old friend Philip Webb.

Since his time, Morris and the work of the Kelmscott Press has been appraised and reappraised; probably there has been more written about him than any other printer. We have him in clearer perspective now, but perhaps we do not admire his work as much as his contemporaries did. The Kelmscott books have been criticized for the heaviness of their types and decorations, for the pomposity of their wide margins. But these were the very qualities that brought his work to notice; they spoke in a loud voice, as it were, and led his contemporaries to see what a fine thing fine printing can be. And the unity of effect in books that Morris insisted upon became a gospel for printers ever since.

The Kelmscott books took time and money to produce; they were expensive to own even then. Museum pieces now, they are locked in glass cases, taken out to be looked at, too precious for extended reading. There is little room in our economy for that kind of individual effort except, perhaps, in the home or in a neighborhood workshop. There is no return. Publishing and the printing industry have been revolutionized by technological advances; books and magazines are now produced at astonishing speed and in fabulous numbers.

Because Morris lived and wrought so well, we no longer turn out books that are a hodgepodge of type styles and a grab-bag of pictures and interloping "decorations" that have no relation to each other or to the page of type. Willy-nilly is out; careful planning is in. By a kind of osmosis, the unifying principles of craftsmanship and fitness to purpose enunciated by William Morris have penetrated the entire field of design. These were his gift to us; they are universal and timeless.

FRIDOLF JOHNSON

Woodstock, New York
February, 1973

ORNAMENTATION
AND
ILLUSTRATIONS FROM
THE
KELMSCOTT
CHAUCER

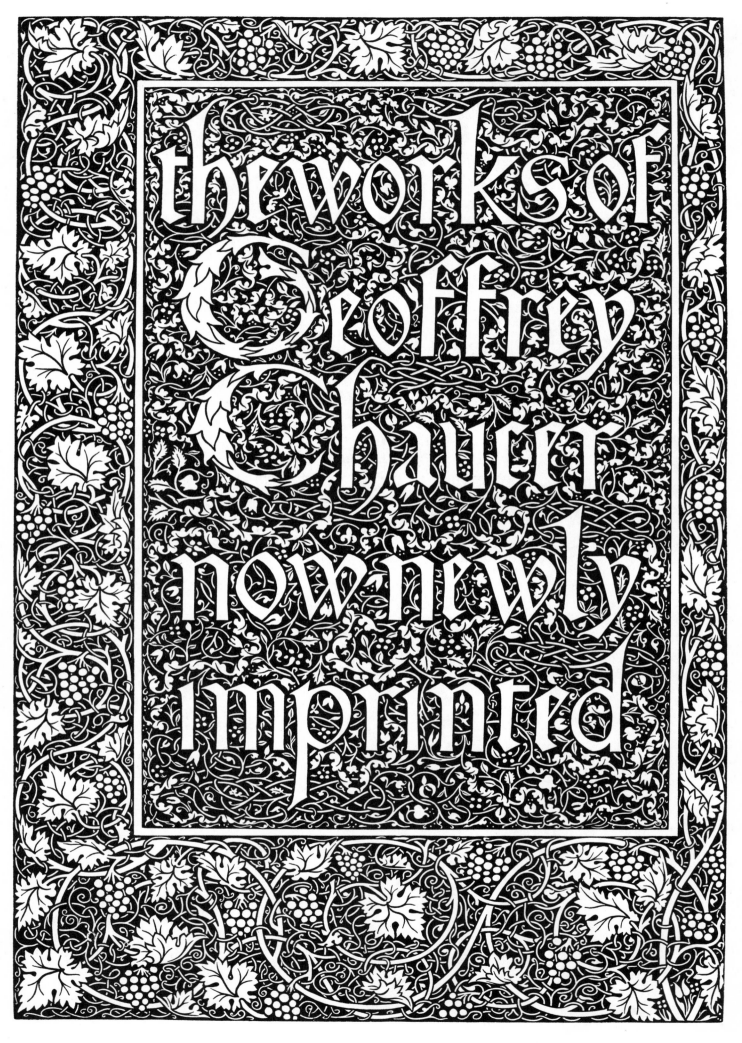

HERE BEGINNETH THE TALES OF CANTER·
BURY AND FIRST THE PROLOGUE THEREOF

WHAN THAT Aprille with his shoures soote
The droghte of March hath perced to the roote,
And bathed every veyne in swich licour,
Of which vertu engendred is the flour;
Whan Zephirus eek with his swete breeth
Inspired hath in every holt and heeth

The tendre croppes, and the yonge sonne
Hath in the Ram his halfe cours yronne,
And smale foweles maken melodye,
That slepen al the nyght with open eye,
So priketh hem nature in hir corages;
Thanne longen folk to goon on pilgrimages,
And palmeres for to seken straunge strondes,
To ferne halwes, kowthe in sondry londes;
And specially, from every shires ende
Of Engelond, to Caunterbury they wende,
The hooly blisful martir for to seke,
That hem hath holpen whan that they were
seke.

BIFIL that in that seson on a day,
In Southwerk at the Tabard as I lay,
Redy to wenden on my pilgrym-
age
To Caunterbury with ful devout
corage,
At nyght were come into that hostelrye
Wel nyne and twenty in a compaignye,
Of sondry folk, by aventure yfalle
In felaweshipe, and pilgrimes were they alle,
That toward Caunterbury wolden ryde.

Two fyres on the auter gan she beete,
And dide hir thynges, as men may biholde
In Stace of Thebes, and thise bookes olde.
Whan kyndled was the fyr, with pitous cheere,
Unto Dyane she spak, as ye may heere.

CHASTE goddesse of the wodes grene,
To whom bothe hevene and erthe & see is sene,
Queene of the regne of Pluto derk and lowe,
Goddesse of maydens, that myn herte hast knowe
ful many a yeer, and woost what I desire,
As keepe me fro thy vengeaunce and thyn ire,
That Attheon aboughte cruelly.
Chaste goddesse, wel wostow that I
Desire to ben a mayden al my lyf,
Ne nevere wol I be no love, ne wyf.
I am, thow woost, yet of thy compaignye
A mayde, and love huntynge and venerye,
And for to walken in the wodes wilde,
And noght to ben a wyf and be with childe;
Noght wol I knowe the compaignye of man.
Now helpe me, lady, sith ye may and kan,
for tho thre formes that thou hast in thee.

And Palamon, that hast swich love to me,
And eek Arcite, that loveth me so soore,
This grace I preye thee withoute moore,
As sende love and pees bitwixe hem two,
And fro me turne awey hir hertes so,
That al hire hoote love and hir desir,
And al hir bisy torment and hir fir,
Be queynt, or turned in another place.
And if so be thou wolt do me no grace,
Or if my destynee be shapen so
That I shal nedes have oon of hem two,
As sende me hym that moost desireth me.
Bihoold, goddesse of clene chastitee,
The bittre teeres that on my chekes falle.
Syn thou art mayde, and kepere of us alle,
My maydenhede thou kepe and wel conserve,
And whil I lyve a mayde, I wol thee serve.
THE fires brenne upon the auter cleere
Whil Emelye was thus in hir preyere;
But sodeynly she saugh a sighte queynte,
for right anon, oon of the fyres queynte
And quyked agayn, and after that, anon
That oother fyr was queynt, and al agon,
And as it queynte it made a whistelynge,
As doon thise wete brondes in hir brennynge;
And at the brondes ende out ran anoon
As it were blody dropes many oon;

for which so soore agast was Emelye,
That she was wel ny mad, and gan to crye,
for she ne wiste what it signyfied;
But oonly for the feere thus hath she cried,
And weepe, that it was pitee for to heere.
And therwithal Dyane gan appeere,
With bowe in honde, right as an hunteresse,
And seyde, Doghter, stynt thyn hevynesse.
Among the goddes hye it is affermed,
And by eterne word writt and confermed,
Thou shalt ben wedded unto oon of tho
That han for thee so muchel care and wo;
But unto which of hem I may nat telle.
farwel, for I ne may no lenger dwelle.
The fires whiche that on myn auter brenne
Shulle thee declaren, er that thou go henne,
Thyn aventure of love, as in this caas.
AND with that word the arwes in the caas
Of the goddesse clateren faste & rynge,
And forth she wente, and made a van-
ysshynge;
for which this Emelye astoned was,
And seyde, What amounteth this, allas!
I putte me in thy proteccioun,
Dyane, and in thy disposicioun.
And hoom she goth anon the nexte weye.
This is theffect, ther is namoore to seye.

THE nexte houre of Mars folwynge this,
Arcite unto the temple walked is
Of fierse Mars, to doon his sacrifise,
With alle the rytes of his payen wyse.
With pitous herte and heigh devocioun,
Right thus to Mars he seyde his orisoun:
O STRONGE god, that
in the regnes colde
Of Trace honoured art
and lord yholde,
And hast in every regne
and every lond
Of armes al the brydel
in thyn hond,
And hem fortunest as
thee lyst devyse,
Accepte of me my pitous sacrifise.
If so be that my youthe may deserve,
And that my myght be worthy for to serve
Thy godhede, that I may been oon of thyne,
Thanne preye I thee to rewe upon my pyne.
for thilke peyne, and thilke hoote fir,
In which thou whilom brendest for desir,
Whan that thou usedeste the beautee
Of faire, yonge, fresshe Venus free,
And haddest hire in armes at thy wille,
Although thee ones on a tyme mysfille,

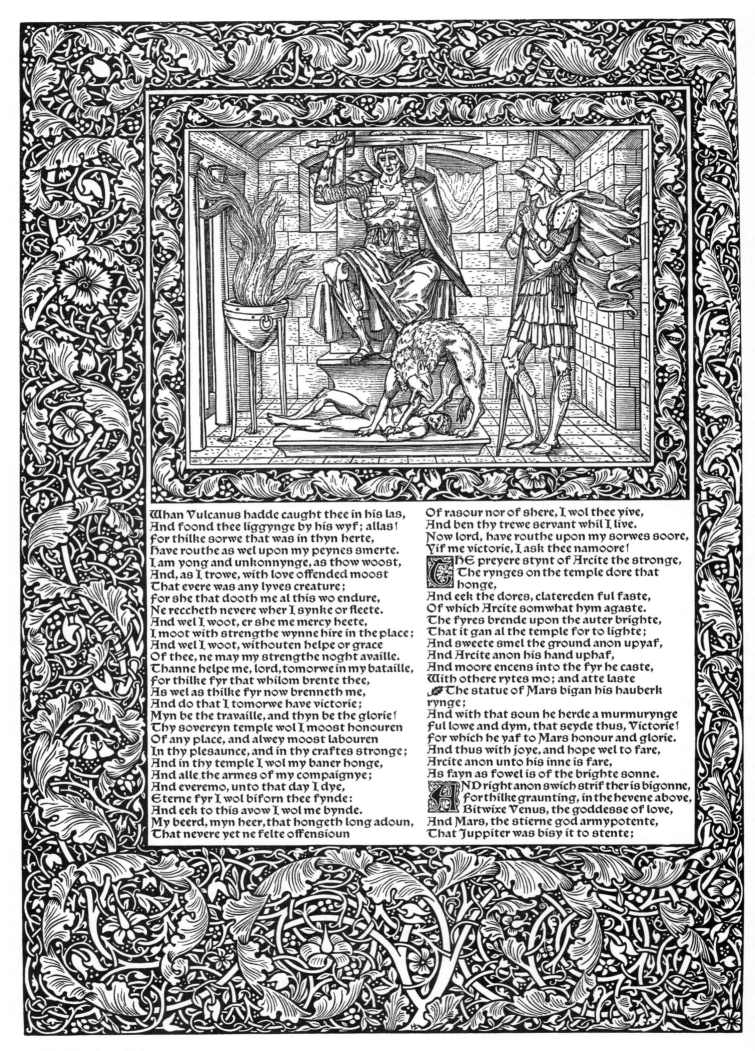

When Vulcanus hadde caught thee in his las,
And foond thee liggynge by his wyf; allas!
for thilke sorwe that was in thyn herte,
Have routhe as wel upon my peynes smerte.
I am yong and unkonnynge, as thow woost,
And, as I trowe, with love offended moost
That evere was any lyves creature;
for she that dooth me al this wo endure,
Ne reccheth nevere wher I synke or fleete.
And wel I woot, er she me mercy heete,
I moot with strengthe wynne hire in the place;
And wel I woot, withouten helpe or grace
Of thee, ne may my strengthe noght availle.
Thanne helpe me, lord, tomorwe in my bataille,
for thilke fyr that whilom brente thee,
As wel as thilke fyr now brenneth me,
And do that I tomorwe have victorie;
Myn be the travaille, and thyn be the glorie!
Thy sovereyn temple wol I moost honouren
Of any place, and alwey moost labouren
In thy plesaunce, and in thy craftes stronge;
And in thy temple I wol my baner honge,
And alle the armes of my compaignye;
And everemo, unto that day I dye,
Eterne fyr I wol biforn thee fynde:
And eek to this avow I wol me bynde.
My beerd, myn heer, that hongeth long adoun,
That nevere yet ne felte offensioun

Of rasour nor of shere, I wol thee yive,
And ben thy trewe servant whil I live.
Now lord, have routhe upon my sorwes soore,
Yif me victorie, I ask thee namoore!
THE preyere stynt of Arcite the stronge,
The rynges on the temple dore that honge,
And eek the dores, clatereden ful faste,
Of which Arcite somwhat hym agaste.
The fyres brende upon the auter brighte,
That it gan al the temple for to lighte;
And sweete smel the ground anon upyaf,
And Arcite anon his hand uphaf,
And moore encens into the fyr he caste,
With othere rytes mo; and atte laste
The statue of Mars bigan his hauberk rynge;
And with that soun he herde a murmurynge
ful lowe and dym, that seyde thus, Victorie!
for which he yaf to Mars honour and glorie.
And thus with joye, and hope wel to fare,
Arcite anon unto his inne is fare,
As fayn as fowel is of the brighte sonne.
AND right anon swich strif ther is bigonne,
for thilke grauntyng, in the hevene above,
Bitwixe Venus, the goddesse of love,
And Mars, the stierne god armypotente,
That Juppiter was bisy it to stente;

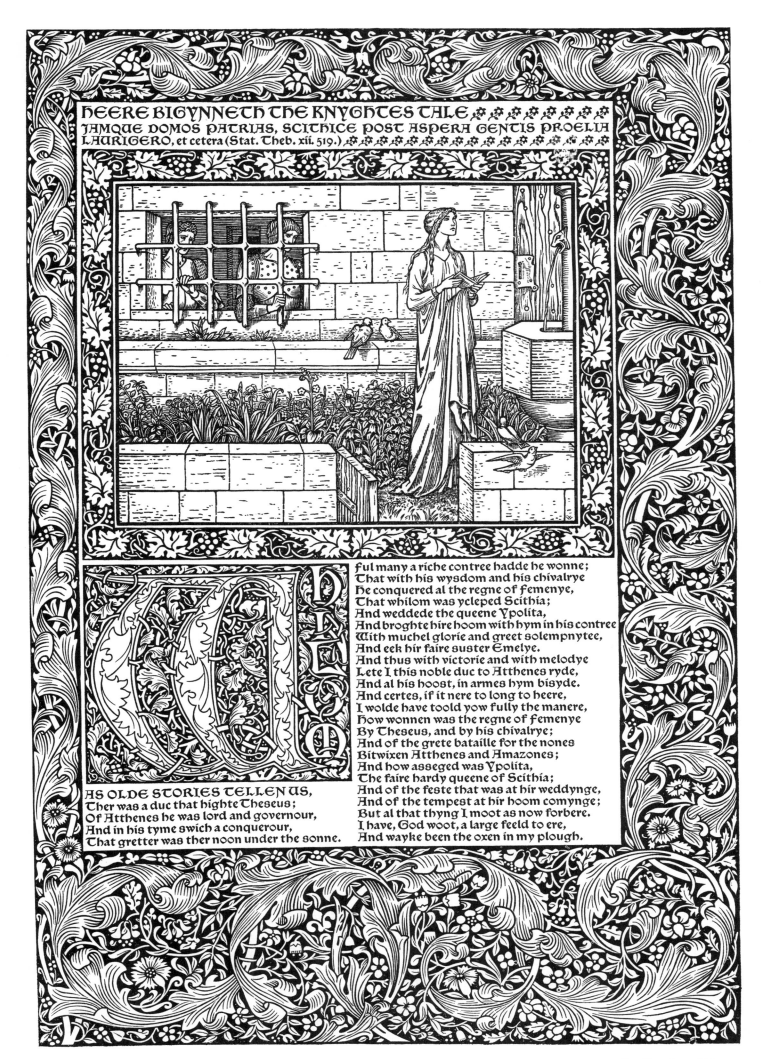

HEERE BIGYNNETH THE KNYGHTES TALE ❧❧❧❧❧❧❧
IAMQUE DOMOS PATRIAS, SCITHICE POST ASPERA GENTIS PROELIA
LAURIGERO, et cetera (Stat. Theb. xii. 519.) ❧❧❧❧❧❧❧❧

Ful many a riche contree hadde he wonne;
That with his wysdom and his chivalrye
He conquered al the regne of Femenye,
That whilom was ycleped Scithia;
And weddede the queene Ypolita,
And broghte hire hoom with hym in his contree
With muchel glorie and greet solempnytee,
And eek hir faire suster Emelye.
And thus with victorie and with melodye
Lete I this noble duc to Atthenes ryde,
And al his hoost, in armes hym bisyde.
And certes, if it nere to long to heere,
I wolde have toold yow fully the manere,
How wonnen was the regne of Femenye
By Theseus, and by his chivalrye;
And of the grete bataille for the nones
Bitwixen Atthenes and Amazones;
And how asseged was Ypolita,
The faire hardy queene of Scithia;
And of the feste that was at hir weddynge,
And of the tempest at hir hoom comynge;
But al that thyng I moot as now forbere.
I have, God woot, a large feeld to ere,
And wayke been the oxen in my plough.

AS OLDE STORIES TELLEN US,
Ther was a duc that highte Theseus;
Of Atthenes he was lord and governour,
And in his tyme swich a conquerour,
That gretter was ther noon under the sonne.

Departed is with duetee and honour
Out of this foule prisoun of this lyf?
Why grucchen heere his cosyn and his wyf
Of his welfare that loved hem so weel?
Kan he hem thank? Nay, God woot, never a deel,
That bothe his soule & eek hemself offende,
And yet they mowe hir lustes nat amende.

WHAT may I conclude of this longe serye,
But after wo, I rede us to be merye,
And thanken Juppiter of al his grace?
And er that we departen from this place,
I rede that we make of sorwes two,
O parfit joye, lastynge everemo.
And looketh now, wher moost sorwe is herinne,
Ther wol we first amenden and bigynne.
Suster, quod he, this is my fulle assent,
With all thavys heere of my parlement,
That gentil Palamon, thyn owene knyght,
That serveth yow with wille, herte, and myght,
And evere hath doon, syn that ye first hym knewe,
That ye shul, of your grace, upon hym rewe,
And taken hym for housbonde and for lord;
Lene me youre hond, for this is oure accord.

Lat se now of youre wommanly pitee;
He is a kynges brother sone, pardee,
And though he were a povre bacheler,
Syn he hath served yow so many a yeer
And had for yow so greet adversitee,
It moste been considered, leeveth me,
For gentil mercy oghte to passen right.

THANNE seyde he thus to Palamon ful right:
I trowe ther nedeth litel sermonyng
To make yow assente to this thyng;
Com neer, and taak youre lady by the hond.
Bitwixen hem was maad anon the bond
That highte matrimoigne, or mariage,
By al the conseil and the baronage.
And thus with alle blisse and melodye
Hath Palamon ywedded Emelye;
And God, that al this wyde world hath wroght,
Sende hym his love, that it deere aboght;
For now is Palamon in alle wele,
Lyvynge in blisse, in richesse, and in heele;
And Emelye hym loveth so tendrely,
And he hire serveth al so gentilly,
That nevere was ther no word hem bitwene
Of jalousie, or any oother tene.
Thus endeth Palamon and Emelye,
And God save al this faire compaignye.
Heere is ended the Knyghtes Tale ✿ ✿

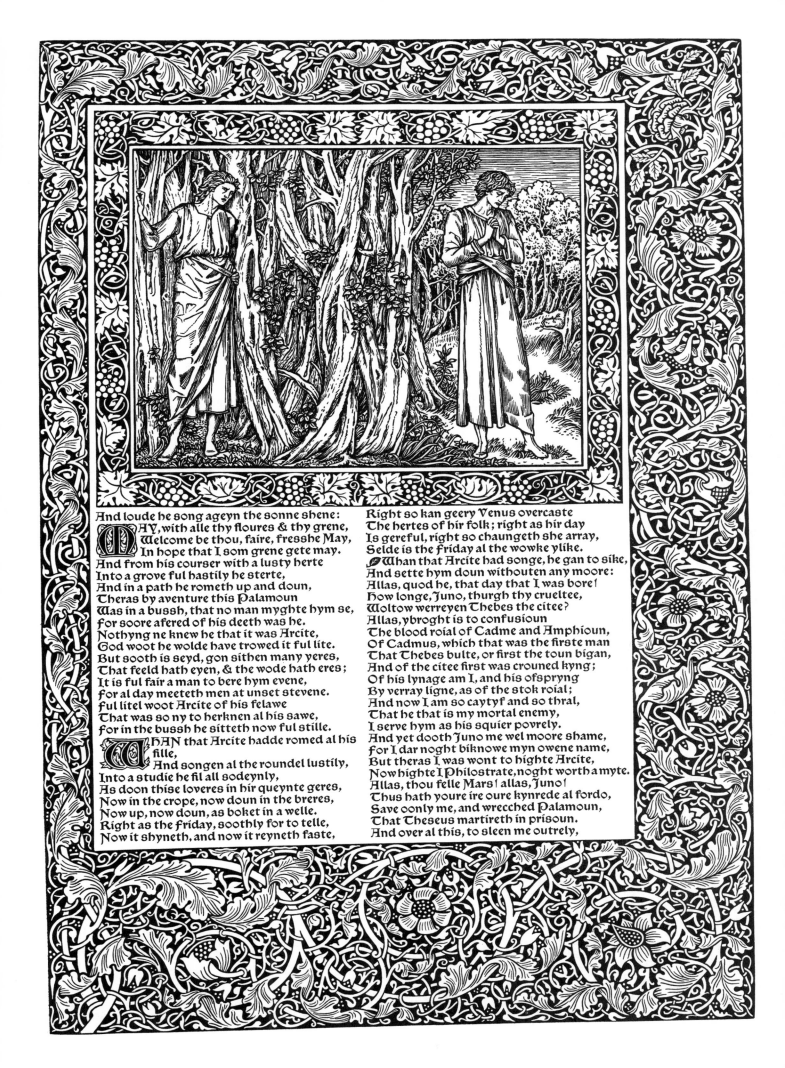

And loude he song ageyn the sonne shene:

Ⓜ AY, with alle thy floures & thy grene,
Welcome be thou, faire, fresshe May,
In hope that I som grene gete may.
And from his courser with a lusty herte
Into a grove ful hastily he sterte,
And in a path he rometh up and doun,
Theras by aventure this Palamoun
Was in a bussh, that no man myghte hym se,
For soore afered of his deeth was he.
Nothyng ne knew he that it was Arcite,
God woot he wolde have trowed it ful lite.
But sooth is seyd, gon sithen many yeres,
That feeld hath eyen, & the wode hath eres;
It is ful fair a man to bere hym evene,
For al day meeteth men at unset stevene.
Ful litel woot Arcite of his felawe
That was so ny to herknen al his sawe,
For in the bussh he sitteth now ful stille.

Ⓦ HAN that Arcite hadde romed al his
fille,
And songen al the roundel lustily,
Into a studie he fil al sodeynly,
As doon thise loveres in hir queynte geres,
Now in the crope, now doun in the breres,
Now up, now doun, as boket in a welle.
Right as the friday, soothly for to telle,
Now it shyneth, and now it reyneth faste,

Right so kan geery Venus overcaste
The hertes of hir folk; right as hir day
Is gereful, right so chaungeth she array,
Selde is the friday al the wowke ylike.

🖛 Whan that Arcite had songe, he gan to sike,
And sette hym doun withouten any moore:
Allas, quod he, that day that I was bore!
How longe, Juno, thurgh thy crueltee,
Woltow werreyen Thebes the citee?
Allas, ybroght is to confusioun
The blood roial of Cadme and Amphioun,
Of Cadmus, which that was the firste man
That Thebes bulte, or first the toun bigan,
And of the citee first was crouned kyng;
Of his lynage am I, and his ofspryng
By verray ligne, as of the stok roial;
And now I am so caytyf and so thral,
That he that is my mortal enemy,
I serve hym as his squier povrely.
And yet dooth Juno me wel moore shame,
For I dar noght biknowe myn owene name,
But theras I was wont to highte Arcite,
Now highte I Philostrate, noght worth a myte.
Allas, thou felle Mars! allas, Juno!
Thus hath youre ire oure kynrede al fordo,
Save oonly me, and wrecched Palamoun,
That Theseus martireth in prisoun.
And over al this, to sleen me outrely,

A litel scole of cristen folk ther stood
Doun at the ferther ende, in which ther were
Children an heepe, ycomen of cristen blood,
That lerned in that scole yeer by yere
Swich manere doctrine as men used there,
This is to seyn, to syngen and to rede,
As smale children doon in hire childhede.

AMONG thise children was a wydwes
sone,
A litel clergeon, seven yeer of age,
That day by day to scole was his wone,
And eek also, whereas he saugh thymage
Of Cristes mooder, hadde he in usage,
As hym was taught, to knele adoun and seye
His Ave Marie, as he goth by the weye.

Thus hath this wydwe hir litel sone ytaught
Oure blisful lady, Cristes mooder deere,
To worshipe ay, and he forgate it naught,
for sely child wol alday soone leere;
But ay, when I remembre on this mateere,
Seint Nicholas stant evere in my presence,
for he so yong to Crist dide reverence.

This litel child, his litel book lernynge,
As he sat in the scole at his prymer,

WAS IN ASYE, IN A GREET CITEE,
Amonges cristene folk, a Jewerye,
Sustened by a lord of that contree
for foule usure, and lucre of vileynye,
Hateful to Crist and to his compaignye;
And thurgh the strete men myghte ride or
wende,
for it was free, and open at eyther ende.

THE PROLOGE OF THE TALE OF THE MANNE OF LAWE ❧ ❧

HARM! CONDICION OF POVERTE!
With thurst, with coold, with hunger so con-
foundid!
To asken help thee shameth in thyn herte;
If thou noon aske, so soore artow ywoundid,
That verray nede unwrappeth al thy wounde
hid!
Maugree thyn heed, thou most for indigence
Or stele, or begge, or borwe thy despence!

Thow blamest Crist, and seist ful bitterly,
He mysdeparteth richesse temporal;
Thy neighebore thou wytest synfully,
And seist thou hast to lite, and he hath al.
Parfay, seistow, somtyme he rekene shal,
Whan that his tayl shal brennen in the gleede,
For he noght helpeth needfulle in hir neede.

Herkne what is the sentence of the wise:
Bet is to dyen than have indigence;
Thyselve neighebor wol thee despise;
If thou be povre, farwel thy reverence!
Yet of the wise man take this sentence:
Alle the dayes of povre men been wikke;
Be war therfore, er thou come to that prikke!

If thou be povre, thy brother hateth thee,
And alle thy freendes fleen from thee, allas!
O riche marchaunts, ful of wele been yee,
O noble, o prudent folk, as in this cas!
Youre bagges been nat filld with ambes as,
But with sys cynk, that renneth for youre
chaunce;
At Christemasse myrie may ye daunce!

Ye seken lond and see for yowre wynnynges;
As wise folk ye knowen al thestaat
Of regnes; ye been fadres of tidynges

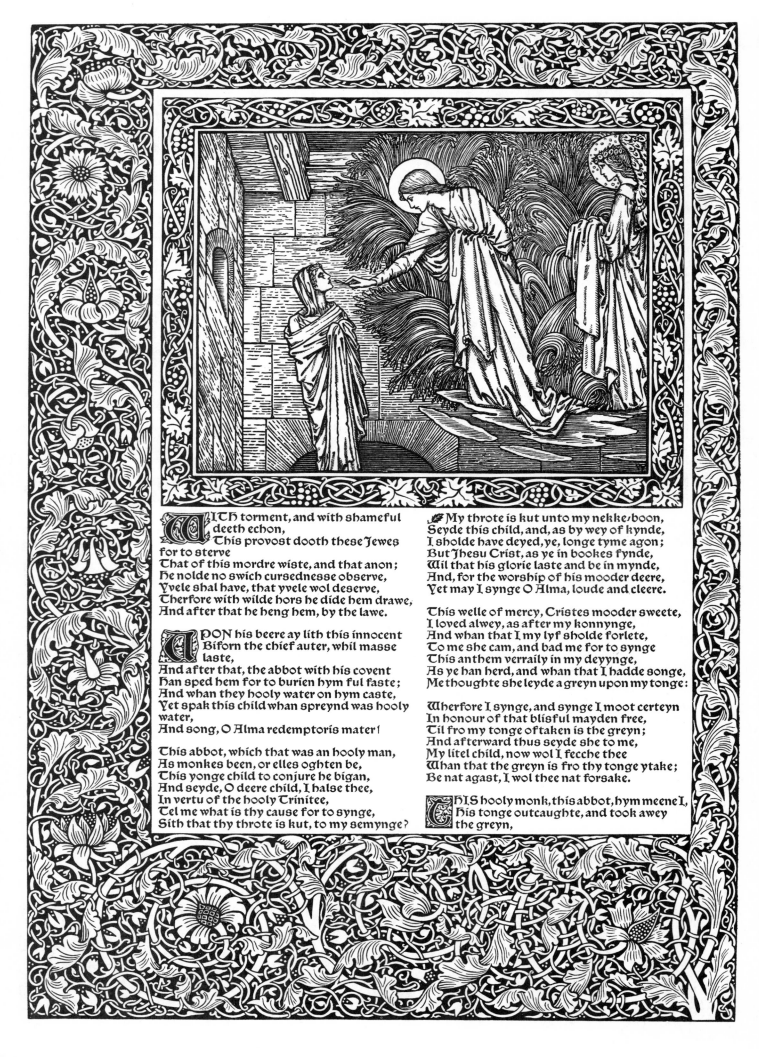

WITH torment, and with shameful
deeth echon,
This provost dooth these Jewes
for to sterve
That of this mordre wiste, and that anon;
He nolde no swich cursednesse observe,
Yvele shal have, that yvele wol deserve,
Therfore with wilde hors he dide hem drawe,
And after that he heng hem, by the lawe.

UPON his beere ay lith this innocent
Biforn the chief auter, whil masse
laste,
And after that, the abbot with his covent
Han sped hem for to burien hym ful faste;
And whan they hooly water on hym caste,
Yet spak this child whan spreynd was hooly
water,
And song, O Alma redemptoris mater!

This abbot, which that was an hooly man,
As monkes been, or elles oghten be,
This yonge child to conjure he bigan,
And seyde, O deere child, I halse thee,
In vertu of the hooly Trinitee,
Tel me what is thy cause for to synge,
Sith that thy throte is kut, to my semynge?

My throte is kut unto my nekke-boon,
Seyde this child, and, as by wey of kynde,
I sholde have deyed, ye, longe tyme agon;
But Jhesu Crist, as ye in bookes fynde,
Wil that his glorie laste and be in mynde,
And, for the worship of his mooder deere,
Yet may I synge O Alma, loude and cleere.

This welle of mercy, Cristes mooder sweete,
I loved alwey, as after my konnynge,
And whan that I my lyf sholde forlete,
To me she cam, and bad me for to synge
This anthem verraily in my deyynge,
As ye han herd, and whan that I hadde songe,
Me thoughte she leyde a greyn upon my tonge:

Wherfore I synge, and synge I moot certeyn
In honour of that blisful mayden free,
Til fro my tonge oftaken is the greyn;
And afterward thus seyde she to me,
My litel child, now wol I fecche thee
Whan that the greyn is fro thy tonge ytake;
Be nat agast, I wol thee nat forsake.

THIS hooly monk, this abbot, hym meene I,
His tonge outcaughte, and took awey
the greyn,

Incipit secunda pars 🌸 🌸 🌸 🌸 🌸 🌸 🌸 🌸

AMONGES thise povre folk ther
dwelte a man
Which that was holden povrest of
hem alle;
But hye God som tyme senden kan
His grace into a litel oxes stalle:
Janicula men of that throop hym calle.
A doghter hadde he, fair ynogh to sighte,
And Grisildis this yonge mayden highte.

But for to speke of vertuous beautee,
Thanne was she oon the faireste under sonne;
For povreliche yfostred up was she,
No likerous lust was thurgh hire herte yronne;
Wel ofter of the welle than of the tonne
She drank, and for she wolde vertu plese,
She knew wel labour, but noon ydel ese.

But thogh this mayde tendre were of age,
Yet in the brest of hire virginitee
Ther was enclosed rype and sad corage,
And in greet reverence and charitee
Hir olde povre fader fostred shee;
A fewe sheep, spynnynge, on feeld she kepte,
She wolde noght been ydel til she slepte.

And whan she homward cam, she wolde brynge
Wortes, or other herbes, tymes ofte,

FER FRO THILKE PALAYS HONUR-
ABLE
Theras this markys shoop his mariage,
Ther stood a throop, of site delitable,
In which that povre folk of that village
Hadden hir beestes and hir herbergage,
And of hire labour tooke hir sustenance,
After that the erthe yaf hem habundance.

The nexte thyng that I requere thee,
Thou shalt it do, if it lye in thy myght;
And I wol telle it yow, er it be nyght.
HAVE heer my trouthe, quod the knyght,
I grante.
O Thanne, quod she, I dar me wel avante
Thy lyf is sauf, for I wol stonde therby,
Upon my lyf, the queene wol seye as I.
Lat se which is the proudeste of hem alle
That wereth on a coverchief or a calle,
That dar seye Nay, of that I shal thee teche.
Lat us go forth withouten lenger speche.
Tho rowned she a pistel in his ere,
And bad hym to be glad and have no fere.
WHAN they be comen to the court,
this knyght
Seyde, he had holde his day, as he
hadde hight,
And redy was his answere, as he sayde.
ful many a noble wyf, and many a mayde,
And many a wydwe, for that they been wise,
The queene hirself sittynge as a justise,
Assembled been, his answere for to heere;
And afterward this knyght was bode appeere.
TO every wight comanded was silence,
And that the knyght sholde telle in
audience,
What thyng that worldly wommen loven best.

This knyght ne stood nat stille as doth a
best,
But to his questioun anon answerde
With manly voys, that al the court it herde:
MY lige lady, generally, quod he,
Wommen desiren have sovereynetee
As wel over hir housbond as hir love,
And for to been in maistrie hym above;
This is youre moost desir, thogh ye me kille.
Dooth as yow list, I am heer at youre wille.
IN al the court ne was ther wyf, ne mayde,
Ne wydwe, that contraried that he
sayde,
But seyden, He was worthy han his lyf;
And with that word up stirte the olde wyf,
Which that the knyght saugh sittynge in the
grene:
Mercy! quod she, my sovereyn lady queene!
Er that youre court departe, do me right;
I taughte this answere unto the knyght;
for which he plighte me his trouthe there,
The firste thyng I wolde of hym requere,
He wolde it do, if it lay in his myght.
Bifore the court thanne preye I thee, sir
knyght,
Quod she, that thou me take unto thy wyf;
for wel thou woost that I have kept thy lyf.
If I sey fals, sey Nay, upon thy fey!

THIS knyght answerde, Allas, and weylawey!
I woot right wel that swich was my biheste.
For Goddes love, as chees a newe requeste!
Taak al my good, and lat my body go.
Nay thanne, quod she, I shrewe us bothe two!
For thogh that I be foul, and oold, and poore,
I nolde for al the metal, ne for oore
That under erthe is grave, or lith above,
But if thy wyf I were, and eek thy love!

MY love? quod he, nay, my dampnacioun!
Allas! that any of my nacioun
Sholde evere so foule disparaged be!
But al for noght, the ende is this, that he
Constreyned was, he nedes moste hire wedde;
And taketh his olde wyf, and gooth to bedde.

NOW wolden som men seye, paraventure,
That, for my necligence, I do no cure
To tellen yow the joye and al tharray,
That at the feeste was that ilke day.
To which thyng shortly answeren I shal;
I seye, ther nas no joye ne feeste at al,
Ther nas but hevynesse, and muche sorwe,
For prively he wedded hire on morwe,
And al day after hidde hym as an owle;

So wo was hym, his wyf looked so foule.
GREET was the wo the knyght hadde in his thoght,
Whan he was with his wyf abedde ybroght.
He walweth, and he turneth to and fro;
His olde wyf lay smylynge everemo,
And seyde, O deere housbonde, benedicitee!
Fareth every knyght thus with his wyf as ye?
Is this the lawe of kyng Arthures hous?
Is every knyght of his so dangerous?
I am youre owene love, and eek youre wyf;
I am she which that saved hath youre lyf,
And certes, yet dide I yow nevere unright.
Why fare ye thus with me this firste nyght?
Ye faren lyk a man had lost his wit;
What is my gilt? For Goddes love tel it,
And it shal been amended, if I may.
Amended! quod this knyght, allas! nay, nay!
It wol nat been amended nevere mo,
Thou art so loothly, and so oold also,
And therto comen of so lough a kynde,
That litel wonder is, thogh I walwe and wynde.
So wolde God, myn herte wolde breste!
Is this, quod she, the cause of youre unreste?
Ye, certeinly, quod he, no wonder is.

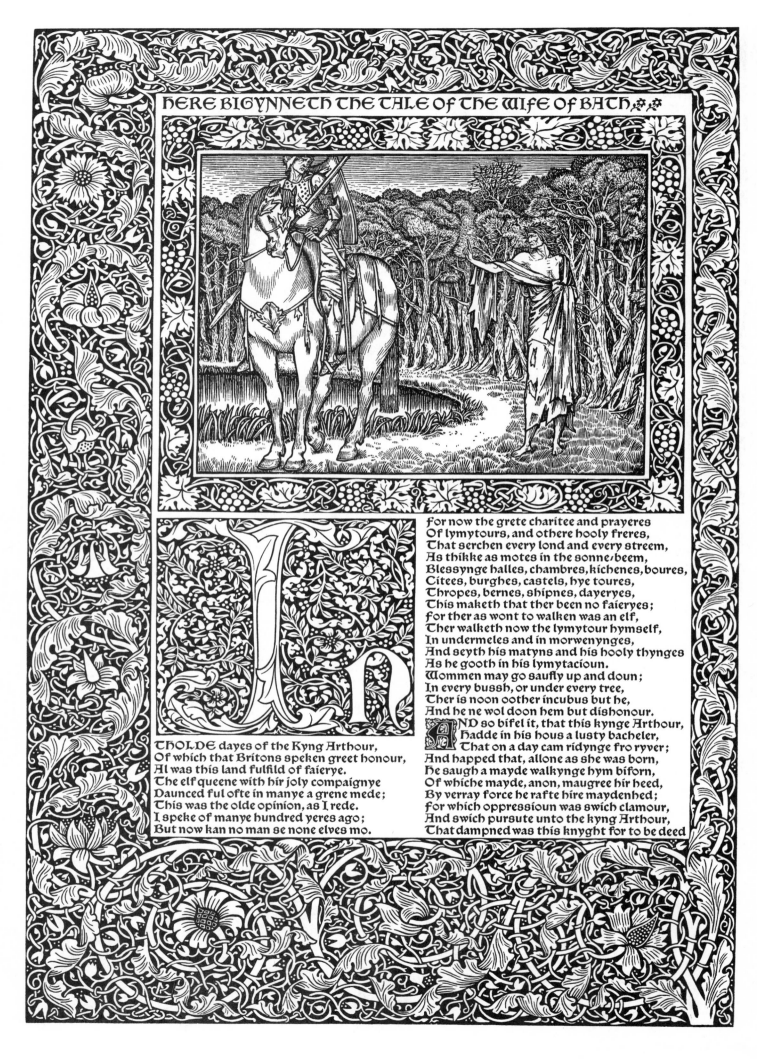

HERE BIGYNNETH THE TALE OF THE WIFE OF BATH.

IN THOLDE dayes of the Kyng Arthour,
Of which that Britons speken greet honour,
Al was this land fulfild of faierye.
The elf queene with hir joly compaignye
Daunced ful ofte in manye a grene mede;
This was the olde opinion, as I rede.
I speke of manye hundred yeres ago;
But now kan no man se none elves mo.

for now the grete charitee and prayeres
Of lymytours, and othere hooly freres,
That serchen every lond and every streem,
As thikke as motes in the sonne-beem,
Blessynge halles, chambres, kichenes, boures,
Citees, burghes, castels, hye toures,
Thropes, bernes, shipnes, dayeryes,
This maketh that ther been no faieryes;
for ther as wont to walken was an elf,
Ther walketh now the lymytour hymself,
In undermeles and in morwenynges,
And seyth his matyns and his hooly thynges
As he gooth in his lymytacioun.
Wommen may go saufly up and doun;
In every bussh, or under every tree,
Ther is noon oother incubus but he,
And he ne wol doon hem but dishonour.
AND so bifel it, that this kynge Arthour,
Hadde in his hous a lusty bacheler,
That on a day cam ridynge fro ryver;
And happed that, allone as she was born,
He saugh a mayde walkynge hym biforn,
Of whiche mayde, anon, maugree hir heed,
By verray force he rafte hire maydenhed;
for which oppressioun was swich clamour,
And swich pursute unto the kyng Arthour,
That dampned was this knyght for to be deed

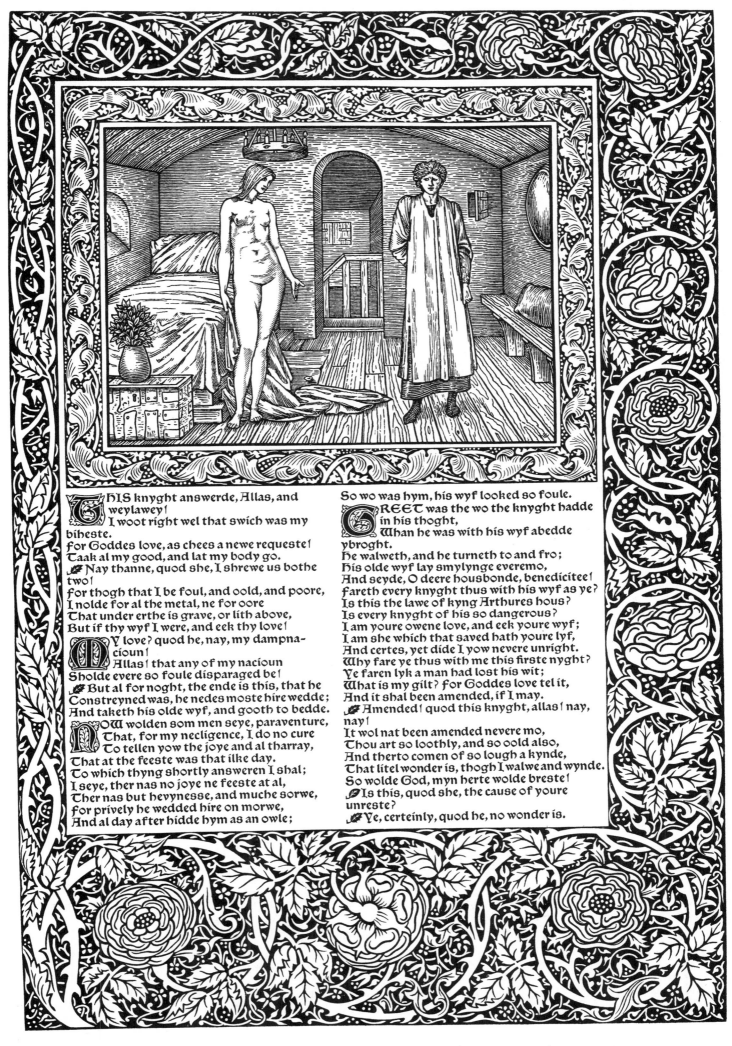

THIS knyght answerde, Allas, and
weylawey!
    I woot right wel that swich was my
biheste.
For Goddes love, as chees a newe requeste!
Taak al my good, and lat my body go.
    Nay thanne, quod she, I shrewe us bothe
two!
For thogh that I be foul, and oold, and poore,
I nolde for al the metal, ne for oore
That under erthe is grave, or lith above,
But if thy wyf I were, and eek thy love!
    MY love? quod he, nay, my dampna-
cioun!
    Allas! that any of my nacioun
Sholde evere so foule disparaged be!
    But al for noght, the ende is this, that he
Constreyned was, he nedes moste hire wedde;
And taketh his olde wyf, and gooth to bedde.
    NOW wolden som men seye, paraventure,
    That, for my necligence, I do no cure
    To tellen yow the joye and al tharray,
That at the feeste was that ilke day.
To which thyng shortly answeren I shal;
I seye, ther nas no joye ne feeste at al,
Ther nas but hevynesse, and muche sorwe,
For prively he wedded hire on morwe,
And al day after hidde hym as an owle;

So wo was hym, his wyf looked so foule.
    GREET was the wo the knyght hadde
    in his thoght,
    Whan he was with his wyf abedde
ybroght.
He walweth, and he turneth to and fro;
His olde wyf lay smylynge everemo,
And seyde, O deere housbonde, benedicitee!
Fareth every knyght thus with his wyf as ye?
Is this the lawe of kyng Arthures hous?
Is every knyght of his so dangerous?
I am youre owene love, and eek youre wyf;
I am she which that saved hath youre lyf,
And certes, yet dide I yow nevere unright.
Why fare ye thus with me this firste nyght?
Ye faren lyk a man had lost his wit;
What is my gilt? For Goddes love tel it,
And it shal been amended, if I may.
    Amended! quod this knyght, allas! nay,
nay!
It wol nat been amended nevere mo,
Thou art so loothly, and so oold also,
And therto comen of so lough a kynde,
That litel wonder is, thogh I walwe and wynde.
So wolde God, myn herte wolde breste!
    Is this, quod she, the cause of youre
unreste?
    Ye, certeinly, quod he, no wonder is.

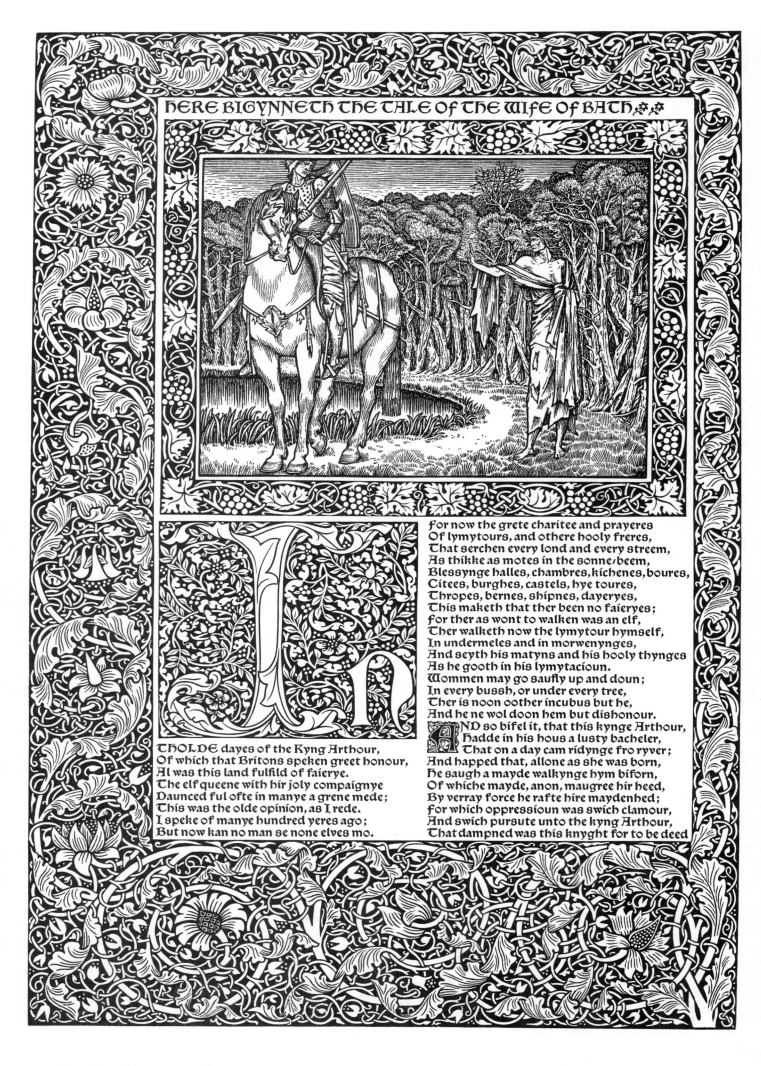

HERE BIGYNNETH THE TALE OF THE WIFE OF BATH.

IN THOLDE dayes of the Kyng Arthour,
Of which that Britons speken greet honour,
Al was this land fulfild of faierye.
The elf queene with hir joly compaignye
Daunced ful ofte in manye a grene mede;
This was the olde opinion, as I rede.
I speke of manye hundred yeres ago;
But now kan no man se none elves mo.

For now the grete charitee and prayeres
Of lymytours, and othere hooly freres,
That serchen every lond and every streem,
As thikke as motes in the sonne-beem,
Blessynge halles, chambres, kichenes, boures,
Citees, burghes, castels, hye toures,
Thropes, bernes, shipnes, dayeryes,
This maketh that ther been no faieryes;
For ther as wont to walken was an elf,
Ther walketh now the lymytour hymself,
In undermeles and in morwenynges,
And seyth his matyns and his hooly thynges
As he gooth in his lymytacioun.
Wommen may go saufly up and doun;
In every bussh, or under every tree,
Ther is noon oother incubus but he,
And he ne wol doon hem but dishonour.
AND so bifel it, that this kynge Arthour,
Hadde in his hous a lusty bacheler,
That on a day cam ridynge fro ryver;
And happed that, allone as she was born,
He saugh a mayde walkynge hym biforn,
Of whiche mayde, anon, maugree hir heed,
By verray force he rafte hire maydenhed;
For which oppressioun was swich clamour,
And swich pursute unto the kyng Arthour,
That dampned was this knyght for to be deed

THER IS, AT THE WEST SYDE OF YTAILLE,
Doun at the roote of Vesulus the colde,
A lusty playne, habundant of vitaille,
Where many a tour & toun thou mayst biholde,
That founded were in time of fadres olde,
And many another delitable sighte,
And Saluces this noble contree highte.

A markys whilom lord was of that londe,
As were his worthy eldres hym bifore;
And obeisant and redy to his honde
Were alle his liges, bothe lasse and moore.
Thus in delit he lyveth, and hath doon yoore,
Biloved and drad, thurgh favour of Fortune,
Bothe of his lordes and of his commune.

Therwith he was, to speke as of lynage,
The gentilleste yborn of Lumbardye;
A fair persone, and strong, and yong of age,
And ful of honour and of curteisye;
Discreet ynogh his contree for to gye,
Save in somme thynges that he was to blame,
And Walter was this yonge lordes name.

I BLAME him thus, that he considereth noght
In tyme comynge what hym myghte bityde;
But in his lust present was al his thoght,
As for to hauke and hunte on every syde;
Wel ny alle othere cures leet he slyde;
And eek he nolde, and that was worst of alle,
Wedde no wyf, for noght that may bifalle.

Oonly that point his peple bar so soore,

Enformed of his wyl, sente his message,
Comaundynge hem swiche bulles to devyse
As to his cruel purpos may suffyse,
How that the pope, as for his peples reste,
Bad hym to wedde another, if hym leste.

I seye, he bad they sholde countrefete
The popes bulles, makynge mencioun
That he hath leve his firste wyf to lete,
As by the popes dispensacioun,
To stynte rancour and dissencioun
Bitwixe his peple and hym; thus seyde the
bulle,
The which they han publiced atte fulle.

The rude peple, as it no wonder is,
Wenden ful wel that it hadde be right so;
But whan thise tidynges cam to Grisildis,
I deeme that hire herte was ful wo.
But she, ylike sad for everemo,
Disposed was, this humble creature,
Thadversitee of fortune al tendure,

Abidynge evere his lust and his plesance
To whom that she was yeven, herte and al,
As to hire verray worldly suffisance;
But shortly if this storie I tellen shal,
This markys writen hath in special
A lettre in which he sheweth his entente,

And secrely he to Boloigne it sente.

To the erl of Panyk, which that hadde tho
Wedded his suster, preyde he specially
To bryngen hoom agayn his children two
In honurable estaat al openly.
But o thyng he hym preyde outrely,
That he to no wight, though men wolde en-
quere,
Sholde nat telle, whos children that they
were,

But seye, the mayden sholde ywedded be
Unto the markys of Saluce anon.
And as this erl was preyed, so dide he;
For at day set he on his wey is goon
Toward Saluce, and lordes many oon
In riche array, this mayden for to gyde,
Hir yonge brother ridynge hire bisyde.

Arrayed was toward hir mariage
This fresshe mayde, ful of gemmes cleere;
Hir brother, which that seven yeer was of age,
Arrayed eek ful fressh in his manere.
And thus in greet noblesse and with glad
cheere,
Toward Saluces shapynge hir journey,
Fro day to day they ryden in hir wey.
Explicit quarta pars.

AL THIS, AFTER HIS WIKKE USAGE,
This markys, yet his wyf to tempte moore
To the outtreste preeve of hir corage,
Fully to han experience and loore
If that she were as stedefast as bifoore,
He on a day, in open audience,
Ful boistously hath seyd hire this sentence:

Certes, Grisilde, I hadde ynogh plesance
To han yow to my wyf for youre goodnesse
As for youre trouthe & for youre obeisance,
Noght for youre lynage ne for youre richesse;
But now knowe I, in verray soothfastnesse,
That in greet lordshipe, if I wel avyse,
Ther is greet servitute in sondry wyse.

I may nat doon as every plowman may;
My peple me constreyneth for to take
Another wyf, and crien day by day;
And eek the pope, rancour for to slake,
Consenteth it, that dar I undertake;
And treweliche thus muche I wol yow seye,
My newe wyf is comynge by the weye.

Be strong of herte, and voyde anon hir place,
And thilke dowere that ye broghten me,
Taak it agayn, I graunte it of my grace;
Retourneth to youre fadres hous, quod he;
No man may alwey han prosperitee;
With evene herte I rede yow tendure
This strook of fortune or of aventure.

AND she answerde agayn in pacience:
My lord, quod she, I woot, and wiste alway
How that bitwixen youre magnificence
And my poverte no wight kan ne may
Maken comparisoun; it is no nay.
I ne heeld me nevere digne in no manere
To be your wyf, no, ne your chamberere.

And in this hous, ther ye me lady maade,
The heighe God take I for my witnesse,
And also wysly he my soule glaade,
I nevere heeld me lady ne maistresse,
But humble servant to youre worthynesse,
And evere shal, whil that my lyf may dure,
Aboven every worldly creature.

That ye so longe of youre benignitee
Han holden me in honour and nobleye,
Wheras I was noght worthy for to bee,
That thonke I God and yow, to whom I preye
Foryelde it yow; ther is namoore to seye.
Unto my fader gladly wol I wende
And with hym dwelle unto my lyves ende.

Ther I was fostred of a child ful smal,
Til I be deed, my lyf ther wol I lede
A wydwe clene, in body, herte and al.
For sith I yaf to yow my maydenhede,
And am youre trewe wyf, it is no drede,
God shilde swich a lordes wyf to take
Another man to housbonde or to make.

And of youre newe wyf, God of his grace
So graunte yow wele and prosperitee:
For I wol gladly yelden hire my place,
In which that I was blisful wont to bee,
For sith it liketh yow, my lord, quod shee,
That whilom weren al myn hertes reste,
That I shal goon, I wol goon whan yow leste.

But theras ye me profre swich dowaire
As I first broghte, it is wel in my mynde
It were my wrecched clothes, nothyng faire,
The whiche to me were hard now for to fynde.
O goode God! how gentil and how kynde
Ye semed by youre speche and youre visage
The day that maked was oure mariage!

But sooth is seyd, algate I fynde it trewe,
For in effect it preved is on me,
Love is noght oold as whan that it is newe.
But certes, lord, for noon adversitee,
To dyen in the cas, it shal nat bee
That evere in word or werk I shal repente
That I yow yaf myn herte in hool entente.

My lord, ye woot that, in my fadres place,
Ye dide me streepe out of my povre wede,
And richely me cladden, of youre grace.
To yow broghte I noght elles, out of drede,
But feith and nakednesse and maydenhede;
And heere agayn my clothyng I restoore,
And eek my weddyng/ryng, for everemoore.

The remenant of youre jueles redy be
Inwith youre chambre, dar I saufly sayn;
Naked out of my fadres hous, quod she,
I cam, and naked moot I turne agayn.
Al youre plesance wol I folwen fayn;
But yet I hope it be nat youre entente
That I smoklees out of youre paleys wente.

Ye koude nat doon so dishoneste a thyng,

That thilke wombe in which youre children leye
Sholde, biforn the peple, in my walkyng,
Be seyn al bare; wherfore I yow preye,
Lat me nat lyk a worm go by the weye:
Remembre yow, myn owene lord so deere,
I was youre wyf, though I unworthy weere.

Wherfore, in guerdon of my maydenhede,
Which that I broghte, and noght agayn I bere,
As voucheth sauf to yeve me, to my meede,
But swich a smok as I was wont to were,
That I therwith may wrye the wombe of here
That was youre wyf; and heer take I my leeve
Of yow, myn owene lord, lest I yow greve.

THE smok, quod he, that thou hast on
thy bak,
Lat it be stille, and bere it forth with
thee.
But wel unnethes thilke word he spak,
But wente his wey for routhe and for pitee.
Biforn the folk hirselven strepeth she,
And in hir smok, with heed and foot al bare,
Toward hir fader hous forth is she fare.

THE folk hire folwe wepynge in hir weye,
And fortune ay they cursen as they
goon;
But she fro wepyng kepte hire eyen dreye,
Ne in this tyme word ne spak she noon.
Hir fader, that this tidynge herde anoon,
Curseth the day and tyme that nature
Shoop hym to been a lyves creature.

For out of doute this olde povre man
Was evere in suspect of hir mariage;
For evere he demed, sith that it bigan,
That whan the lord fulfild hadde his corage,

FRO
BOLOIGNE IS THIS ERL OF PANYK
COME,
Of which the fame up sprang to moore and
lesse,
And in the peples eres alle and some

Hym wolde thynke it were a disparage
To his estaat so lowe for to lighte,
And voyden hire as soone as ever he myghte.

AGAYNS his doghter hastiliche goth he,
for he by noyse of folk knew hire
comynge,
And with hire olde coote, as it myghte be,
He covered hire, ful sorwefully wepynge;
But on hire body myghte he it nat brynge,
For rude was the clooth, and moore of age
By dayes fele than at hire mariage.

Thus with hire fader, for a certeyn space,
Dwelleth this flour of wyfly pacience,
That neither by hire wordes ne hire face
Biforn the folk, ne eek in hire absence,
Ne shewed she that hire was doon offence;
Ne of hire heighe estaat no remembraunce
Ne hadde she, as by hire contenaunce.

No wonder is, for in hire grete estaat
Hire goost was evere in pleyn humylitee;
No tendre mouth, noon herte delicaat,
No pompe, no semblant of roialtee;
But ful of pacient benyngnytee,
Discreet and pridelees, ay honurable,
And to hire housbonde evere meke & stable.

Men speke of Job, and moost for his hum-
blesse,
As clerkes, whan hem list, konne wel endite,
Namely of men, but as in soothfastnesse,
Though clerkes preise wommen but a lite,
Ther kan no man in humblesse hym acquite
As womman kan, ne kan been half so trewe
As wommen been, but it be falle of newe.
Explicit quinta pars. Sequitur pars sexta.

Was kouth eek, that a newe markysesse
He with hym broghte, in swich pompe and
richesse,
That nevere was ther seyn with mannes eye
So noble array in al West Lumbardye.

The markys, which that shoop and knew al
this,
Er that this erl was come, sente his message
For thilke sely povre Grisildis;
And she with humble herte and glad visage,
Nat with no swollen thoght in hire corage,
Cam at his heste, and on hire knees hire
sette,
And reverently and wisely she hym grette.

GRISILDE, quod he, my wyl is outrely
This mayden that shal wedded been
to me,
Received be tomorwe as roially
As it possible is in myn hous to be,
And eek that every wight in his degree
Have his estaat in sittyng and servyse
And heigh plesaunce, as I kan best devyse.

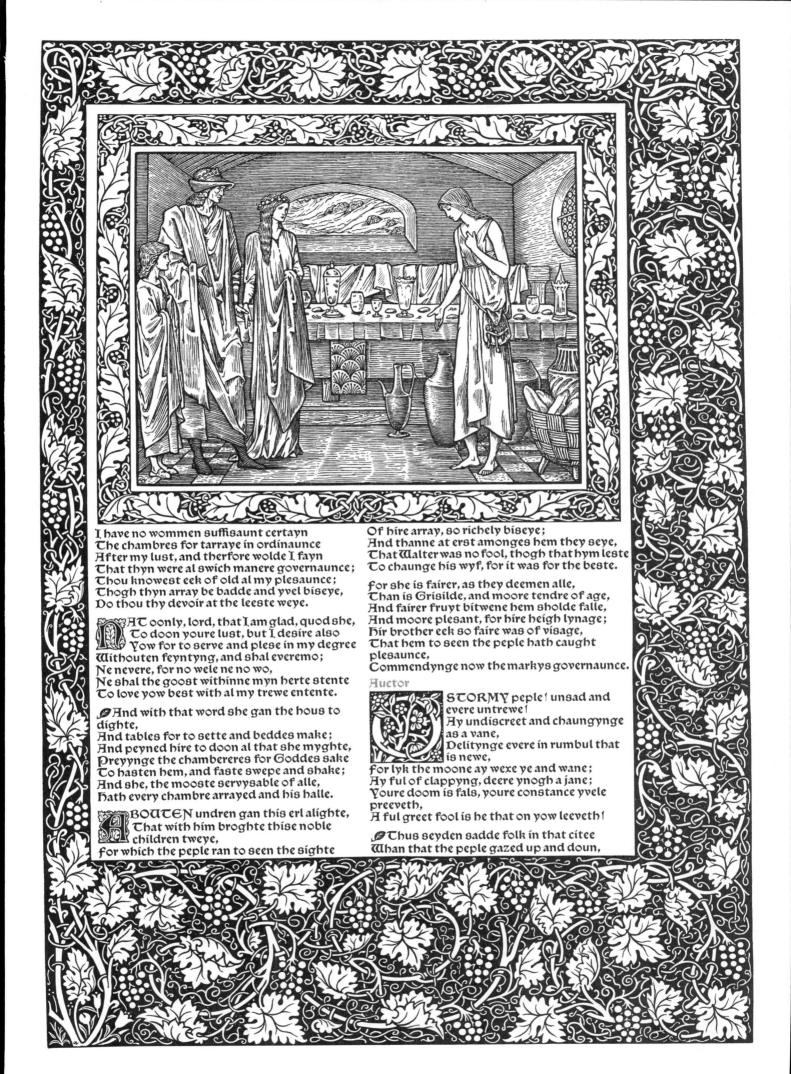

I have no wommen suffisaunt certayn
The chambres for tarraye in ordinaunce
After my lust, and therfore wolde I fayn
That thyn were al swich manere governaunce;
Thou knowest eek of old al my plesaunce;
Thogh thyn array be badde and yvel biseye,
Do thou thy devoir at the leeste weye.

NAT oonly, lord, that I am glad, quod she,
To doon youre lust, but I desire also
Yow for to serve and plese in my degree
Withouten feyntyng, and shal everemo;
Ne nevere, for no wele ne no wo,
Ne shal the goost withinne myn herte stente
To love yow best with al my trewe entente.

And with that word she gan the hous to dighte,
And tables for to sette and beddes make;
And peyned hire to doon al that she myghte,
Preyynge the chambereres for Goddes sake
To hasten hem, and faste swepe and shake;
And she, the mooste servysable of alle,
Hath every chambre arrayed and his halle.

ABOUTEN undren gan this erl alighte,
That with him broghte thise noble children tweye,
For which the peple ran to seen the sighte

Of hire array, so richely biseye;
And thanne at erst amonges hem they seye,
That Walter was no fool, thogh that hym leste
To chaunge his wyf, for it was for the beste.

For she is fairer, as they deemen alle,
Than is Grisilde, and moore tendre of age,
And fairer fruyt bitwene hem sholde falle,
And moore plesant, for hire heigh lynage;
Hir brother eek so faire was of visage,
That hem to seen the peple hath caught plesaunce,
Commendynge now the markys governaunce.

Auctor

STORMY peple! unsad and evere untrewe!
Ay undiscreet and chaungynge as a vane,
Delitynge evere in rumbul that is newe,
For lyk the moone ay wexe ye and wane;
Ay ful of clappyng, deere ynogh a jane;
Youre doom is fals, youre constance yvele preeveth,
A ful greet fool is he that on yow leeveth!

Thus seyden sadde folk in that citee
Whan that the peple gazed up and doun,

Ye maze, maze, goode sire, quod she;
This thank have I for I have maad yow see;
Allas! quod she, that evere I was so kynde!
Now, dame, quod he, lat al passe out of mynde.
Com doun, my lief, and if I have myssayd,
God help me so, as I am yvele apayd.
But, by my fader soule! I wende han seyn,
How that this Damyan had by thee leyn,
And that thy smok had leyn upon his brest.
Ye, sire, quod she, ye may wene as yow lest;
But, sire, a man that waketh out of his sleep,
He may nat sodeynly wel taken keep
Upon a thyng, ne seen it parfitly,
Til that he be adawed verraily;
Right so a man, that longe hath blynd ybe,
Ne may nat sodeynly so wel yse,
First whan his sighte is newe come ageyn,
As he that hath a day or two yseyn,
Til that youre sighte ysatled be a while,
Ther may ful many a sighte yow bigile.
Beth war, I prey yow; for, by hevene kyng,
Ful many a man weneth to seen a thyng,
And it is al another than it semeth.
He that mysconceyveth, he mysdemeth.
And with that word she leep doun fro the tree.
This Januarie, who is glad but he?
He kisseth hire, and clippeth hire ful ofte,
And on hire wombe he stroketh hire ful softe;
And to his palays hoom he hath hire lad.
Now, goode men, I pray yow to be glad.
Thus endeth heere my tale of Januarie;
God blesse us, and his mooder Seinte Marie!
Heere is ended the Marchantes Tale of Januarie.

Words of the Host to the Squire

Y! Goddes mercy!
seyde oure Hoost tho,
Now swich a wyf I
pray God kepe me fro!
Lo, whiche sleightes
and subtilitees
In wommen been! for
ay as bisy as bees
Been they, us sely men
for to deceyve;
And from a sothe evere wol they weyve.
By this Marchauntes tale it preveth weel.
But douteles, as trewe as any steel
I have a wyf, though that she povre be;
But of hir tonge a labbyng shrewe is she,
And yet she hath an heep of vices mo;
Therof no fors, lat alle swiche thynges go.
But wyte ye what? In conseil be it seyd,
Me reweth soore I am unto hire teyd;
For, and I sholde rekenen every vice
Which that she hath, ywis, I were to nyce,
And cause why; it sholde reported be
And toold to hire of somme of this meynee;
Of whom, it nedeth nat for to declare,
Syn wommen konnen outen swich chaffare;
And eek my wit suffiseth nat therto
To tellen al; wherfore my tale is do.
SQUIER, come neer, if it youre wille be,
And sey somwhat of love; for certes, ye
Konnen theron as muche as any man.
Nay, sir, quod he, but I wol seye as I kan
With hertly wyl; for I wol nat rebelle
Agayn youre lust; a tale wol I telle.
Have me excused, if I speke amys,
My wyl is good; and lo, my tale is this.

HEERE BIGYNNETH THE SQUIERES TALE

Incipit prima pars

Thurgh which ther deyde many a doughty man.
This noble kyng was cleped Cambynskan,
Which in his tyme was of so greet renoun
That ther was nowher in no regioun
So excellent a lord in alle thyng;
Hym lakked noght that longeth to a kyng.
As of the secte of which that he was born
He kepte his lay, to which that he was sworn;
And therto he was hardy, wys, and riche,
And piëtous and just, alwey yliche;
Sooth of his word, benigne and honurable,
Of his corage as any centre stable;
Yong, fressh, and strong, in armes desirous
As any bacheler of al his hous.
A fair persone he was, and fortunat,
And kepte alwey so wel roial estat
That ther was nowher swich another man.
This noble kyng, this Tartre Cambynskan
Hadde two sones on Elpheta his wyf,
Of whiche the eldeste highte Algarsyf,

SARRAY, IN THE LAND Of Tartarye,
Ther dwelte a kyng, that werreyed Russye,

That oother sone was cleped Cambalo.
A doghter hadde this worthy kyng also,
That yongest was, and highte Canacee.
But for to telle yow al hir beautee
It lyth nat in my tonge nyn my konnyng;
I dar nat undertake so heigh a thyng.
Myn Englissh eek is insufficient;
It moste been a rethor excellent
That koude his colours longynge for that art,
If he sholde hire discryven every part.
I am noon swich, I moot speke as I kan.
⟡And so bifel that, whan this Cambynskan
Hath twenty wynter born his diademe,
As he was wont fro yeer to yeer, I deme,
He leet the feeste of his nativitee
Doon cryen thurghout Sarray his citee,
The last Idus of March, after the yeer.
℘HEBUS, the sonne, ful joly was and
      cleer,
      For he was neigh his exaltacioun
In Martes face, and in his mansioun
In Aries, the colerik hoote signe.
Ful lusty was the weder and benigne,
For which the fowles, agayn the sonne sheene,
What for the sesoun and the yonge grene,
Ful loude songen hire affecciouns;
Hem semed han geten hem protecciouns
Agayn the swerd of wynter keene and coold.

⟡This Cambynskan, of which I have yow
toold,
In roial vestiment sit on his deys,
With diademe, ful heighe in his paleys,
And halt his feeste, so solempne & so ryche,
That in this world ne was ther noon it lyche.
Of which if I shal tellen al tharray,
Thanne wolde it occupie a someres day;
And eek it nedeth nat for to devyse
At every cours the ordre of hire servyse.
I wol nat tellen of hir strange sewes,
Ne of hir swannes, ne of hire heronsewes.
Eek in that lond, as tellen knyghtes olde,
Ther is som mete that is ful deynte holde
That in this lond men recche of it but smal;
Ther nys no man that may reporten al.
⟡I wol nat taryen yow, for it is pryme,
And for it is no fruyt but los of tyme;
Unto my firste I wole have my recours.
⟡ND so bifel that, after the thridde cours,
      Whil that this kyng sit thus in his
      nobleye,
Herknynge his mynstralles hir thynges pleye
Biforn hym at the bord deliciously,
In at the halle/dore, al sodeynly,
Ther cam a knyght upon a steede of bras,
And in his hand a brood mirour of glas.
Upon his thombe he hadde of gold a ring,

THISE olde gentil
Britons in hir dayes
Of diverse aventures
maden layes,
Rymeyed in hir firste
Briton tonge;
Whiche layes with hir
instruments they
songe,
Or elles redden hem for
hir plesaunce;
And oon of hem have I in remembraunce,
Which I shal seyn with good wyl as I kan.

But, sires, bycause I am a burel man,
At my bigynnyng first I yow biseche,
Have me excused of my rude speche.
I lerned nevere rethorik certeyn;
Thyng that I speke, it moot be bare and
pleyn.
I sleep nevere on the Mount of Pernaso,
Ne lerned Marcus Tullius Cithero.
Colours ne knowe I none, withouten drede,
But swiche colours as growen in the mede,
Or elles swiche as men dye or peynte.
Colours of rethoryk been me to queynte;
My spirit feeleth noght of swich mateere,
But if yow list, my tale shul ye heere.

HEERE BIGYNNETH THE FRANKELEYNS TALE ❀ ❀ ❀ ❀ ❀

IN ARMORIK, that called is Britayne,
Ther was a knyght that loved and dide his
payne
To serve a lady in his beste wise;
And many a labour, many a greet emprise
He for his lady wroghte, er she were wonne;
For she was oon, the faireste under sonne,
And eek therto come of so heigh kynrede,
That wel unnethes dorste this knyght, for
drede,
Telle hire his wo, his peyne, & his distresse.
But atte laste, she, for his worthynesse,
And namely for his meke obeysaunce,
Hath swich a pitee caught of his penaunce,
That pryvely she fil of his accord,
To take hym for hir housbonde and hir lord,
Of swich lordshipe as men han over hir
wyves;
And for to lede the moore in blisse hir lyves,
Of his free wyl he swoor hire as a knyght,
That nevere in al his lyf he, day ne nyght,
Ne sholde upon hym take no maistrie
Agayn hir wyl, ne kithe hire jalousie;
But hire obeye, and folwe hir wyl in al,
As any lovere to his lady shal;
Save that the name of soveraynetee,
That wolde he have, for shame of his degree.

SHE thanked hym, and with ful greet
humblesse,
She seyde, Sire, sith of youre gentillesse
Ye profre me to have so large a reyne,
Ne wolde nevere God bitwixe us tweyne,
As in my gilt, were outher werre or stryf.
Sire, I wol be youre humble trewe wyf;
Have heer my trouthe, til that myn herte breste.
Thus been they bothe in quiete & in reste.

FOR o thyng, sires, saufly dar I seye,
That freendes everych oother moot
obeye,
If they wol longe holden compaignye.
Love wol nat been constreyned by maistrye;
Whan maistrie comth, the god of love anon
Beteth his wynges, and farewel! he is gon!
Love is a thyng as any spirit free;
Wommen of kynde desiren libertee,
And nat to been constreyned as a thral;
And so doon men, if I sooth seyen shal.
Looke, who that is moost pacient in love,
He is at his avantage al above.
Pacience is an heigh vertu certeyn;
For it venquysseth, as thise clerkes seyn,
Thynges that rigour sholde nevere atteyne.
For every word men may nat chide or pleyne.
Lerneth to suffre, or elles so moot I goon,
Ye shul it lerne, wherso ye wole or noon;
For in this world, certein, ther no wight is
That he ne dooth or seith somtyme amys.
Ire, siknesse, or constellacioun,
Wyn, wo, or chaungynge of complexioun,
Causeth ful ofte to doon amys or speken.
On every wrong a man may nat be wreken;
After the tyme moste be temperaunce
To every wight that kan on governaunce.
And therfore hath this wise worthy knyght,
To lyve in ese, suffrance hire bihight,
And she to hym ful wisly gan to swere
That nevere sholde ther be defaute in here.

HEERE may men seen an humble wys
accord;
Thus hath she take hir servant and hir
lord,
Servant in love, and lord in mariage,

Thanne was he bothe in lordship and servage;
Servage? nay, but in lordshipe above,
Sith he hath bothe his lady and his love;
His lady, certes, and his wyf also,
The which that lawe of love acordeth to.
And whan he was in this prosperitee,
Hoom with his wyf he gooth to his contree,
Nat fer fro Penmark, ther his dwellyng was,
Wheras he lyveth in blisse and in solas.

WHO koude telle, but he hadde wedded be,
The joye, the ese, and the prosperitee
That is bitwixe an housbonde & his wyf?
A YEER & moore lasted this blisful lyf,
Til that the knyght of which I speke of thus,
That of Kayrrud was cleped Arveragus,
Shoop hym to goon & dwelle a yeer or tweyne
In Engelond, that cleped was eek Briteyne,
To seke in armes worship and honour,
For al his lust he sette in swich labour;
And dwelled there two yeer, the book seith thus.

NOW wol I stynte of this Arveragus,
And speken I wole of Dorigene his wyf,
That loveth hire housbonde as hire hertes lyf.

For his absence wepeth she and siketh,
As doon thise noble wyves whan hem liketh.
She moorneth, waketh, wayleth, fasteth, pleyneth;
Desir of his presence hire so distreyneth,
That al this wyde world she sette at noght.
Hire freendes, whiche that knewe hir hevy thoght,
Conforten hire in al that ever they may;
They prechen hire, they telle hire nyght and day,
That causelees she sleeth hirself, allas!
And every confort possible in this cas
They doon to hire with al hire bisynesse,
Al for to make hire leve hire hevynesse.

BY proces, as ye knowen everichoon,
Men may so longe graven in a stoon
Til som figure therinne emprented be.
So longe han they conforted hire, til she
Receyved hath, by hope and by resoun,
The emprentyng of hire consolacioun,
Thurgh which hir grete sorwe gan aswage;
She may nat alwey duren in swich rage.

AND eek Arveragus, in al this care,
Hath sent hire lettres hoom of his welfare,
And that he wol come hastily agayn;

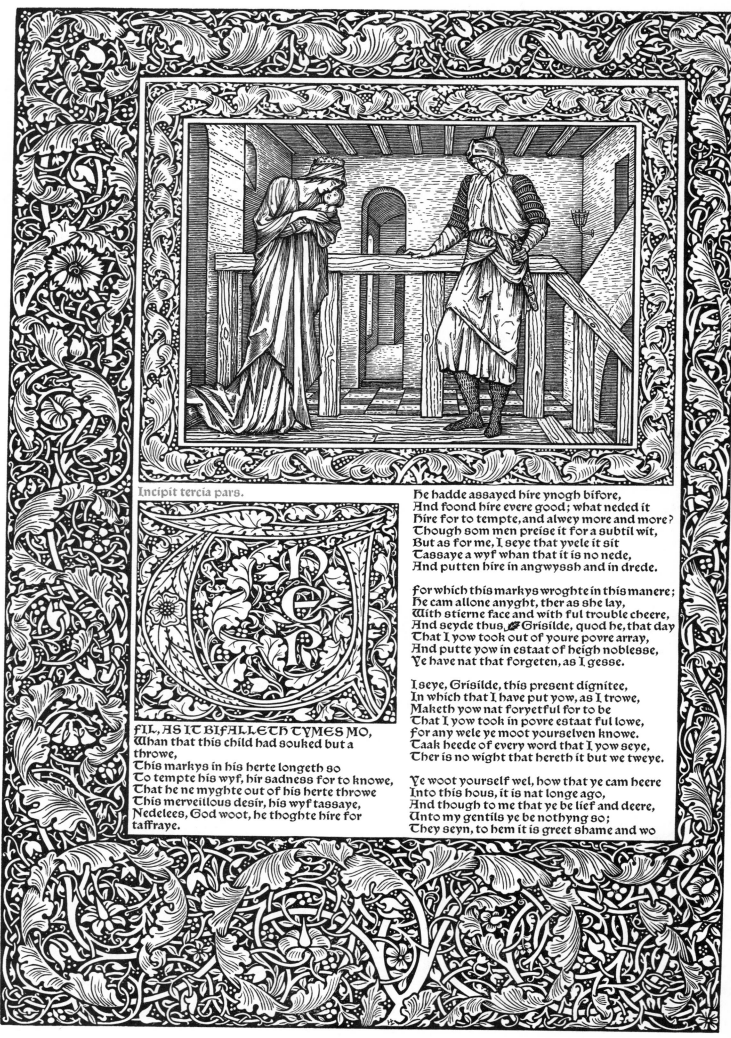

Incipit tercia pars.

He hadde assayed hire ynogh bifore,
And foond hire evere good; what neded it
Hire for to tempte, and alwey more and more?
Though som men preise it for a subtil wit,
But as for me, I seye that yvele it sit
Tassaye a wyf whan that it is no nede,
And putten hire in angwyssh and in drede.

for which this markys wroghte in this manere;
He cam allone anyght, ther as she lay,
With stierne face and with ful trouble cheere,
And seyde thus, "Grisilde, quod he, that day
That I yow took out of youre povre array,
And putte yow in estaat of heigh noblesse,
Ye have nat that forgeten, as I gesse.

I seye, Grisilde, this present dignitee,
In which that I have put yow, as I trowe,
Maketh yow nat foryetful for to be
That I yow took in povre estaat ful lowe,
For any wele ye moot yourselven knowe.
Taak heede of every word that I yow seye,
Ther is no wight that hereth it but we tweye.

Ye woot yourself wel, how that ye cam heere
Into this hous, it is nat longe ago,
And though to me that ye be lief and deere,
Unto my gentils ye be nothyng so;
They seyn, to hem it is greet shame and wo

FIL, AS IT BIFALLETH TYMES MO,
Whan that this child had souked but a
throwe,
This markys in his herte longeth so
To tempte his wyf, hir sadness for to knowe,
That he ne myghte out of his herte throwe
This merveillous desir, his wyf tassaye,
Nedelees, God woot, he thoghte hire for
taffraye.

It may wel be he looked on hir face
In swich a wise, as man that asketh grace;
But nothyng wiste she of his entente.
Nathelees, it happed, er they thennes wente,
Bycause that he was hire neighebour,
And was a man of worship and honour,
And hadde yknowen hym of tyme yoore,
They fille in speche; and forth moore and
moore
Unto his purpos drough Aurelius,
And whan he saugh his tyme, he sayde thus:

MADAME, quod he, by God that this
world made,
So that I wiste it myghte youre herte
glade,
I wolde, that day that youre Arveragus
Wente over the see, that I, Aurelius,
Hadde went ther nevere I sholde have come
agayn;
For wel I woot my servyce is in vayn.
My guerdoun is but brestyng of myn herte;
Madame, reweth upon my peynes smerte;
For with a word ye may me sleen or save,
Heere at youre feet God wolde that I were
grave!
I ne have as now no leyser moore to seye;
Have mercy, sweete, or ye wol do me deye!

SHE gan to looke upon Aurelius:
Is this your wyl, quod she, and sey ye
thus?
Nevere erst, quod she, ne wiste I what ye
mente;
But now, Aurelie, I knowe youre entente,
By thilke God that yaf me soule and lyf,
Ne shal I nevere been untrewe wyf
In word ne werk; as fer as I have wit,
I wol been his to whom that I am knyt!
Taak this for fynal answere as of me.
But after that in pley thus seyde she:
Aurelie, quod she, by heighe God above!
Yet wolde I graunte yow to been youre love,
Syn I yow se so pitously complayne;
Looke what day that, endelong Britayne,
Ye remoeve alle the rokkes, stoon by stoon,
That they ne lette ship ne boot to goon,
I seye, whan ye han maad the coost so clene
Of rokkes, that ther nys no stoon ysene,
Thanne wol I love yow best of any man;
Have heer my trouthe in al that evere I kan!

IS ther noon oother grace in yow? quod
he.
No, by that Lord, quod she, that
maked me!
For wel I woot that it shal never bityde.

And whos child that it was he bad hir hyde
From every wight, for oght that may bityde.

The sergeant gooth, and hath fulfild this
thyng;
But to this markys now retourne we;
For now gooth he ful faste ymaginyng
If by his wyves cheere he myghte se,
Or by hire word aperceyve that she
Were chaunged; but he nevere hire koude fynde

But evere in oon ylike sad and kynde.

As glad, as humble, as bisy in servyse,
And eek in love, as she was wont to be,
Was she to hym in every maner wyse;
Ne of hir doghter noght a word spak she.
Noon accident for noon adversitee
Was seyn in hire, ne nevere hir doghter name
Ne nempned she, in ernest nor in game.
Explicit tercia pars. Sequitur pars quarta.

THIS ESTAAT ther passed been foure yeer
Er she with childe was; but, as God wolde,
A knave child she bar by this Walter,
Ful gracious and fair for to biholde.
And whan that folk it to his fader tolde,
Nat oonly he, but al his contree, merye
Was for this child, and God they thanke and
herye.

Whan it was two yeer old, and fro the brest
Departed of his norice, on a day
This markys caughte yet another lest
To tempte his wyf yet ofter, if he may.
O nedelees was she tempted in assay!
But wedded men ne knowe no mesure,
Whan that they fynde a pacient creature.

Wyf, quod this markys, ye han herd er this,
My peple sikly berth oure mariage,

Seken in every halke and every herne
Particuler sciences for to lerne,
He hym remembred, that upon a day,
At Orliens in studie a book he say
Of magyk natureel, which his felawe,
That was that time a bacheler of lawe,
Al were he ther to lerne another craft,
Hadde prively upon his desk ylaft;
Which book spak muchel of the operaciouns
Touchynge the eighte and twenty mansiouns
That longen to the moone, and swich folye,
As in oure dayes is nat worth a flye;
For hooly chirches feith in oure bileve,
Ne suffreth noon illusion us to greve.
And whan this book was in his remembraunce,
Anon for joye his herte gan to daunce,
And to hymself he seyde pryvely:
My brother shal be warisshed hastily;
For I am siker that ther be sciences
By whiche men make diverse apparences,
Swiche as thise subtile tregetoures pleye.
For ofte at feestes have I wel herd seye,
That tregetours, withinne an halle large,
Have maad come in a water and a barge,
And in the halle rowen up and doun.
Somtyme hath semed come a grym leoun;
And somtyme floures sprynge as in a mede;
Somtyme a vyne, and grapes white and rede;

Somtyme a castel, al of lym and stoon;
And whan hym lyked, voyded it anoon.
Thus semed it to every mannes sighte.
Now thanne conclude I thus, that if I myghte
At Orliens som oold felawe yfynde,
That hadde this moones mansions in mynde,
Or oother magyk natureel above,
He sholde wel make my brother han his love.
For with an apparence a clerk may make
To mannes sighte, that alle the rokkes blake
Of Britaigne weren yvoyded everichon,
And shippes by the brynke comen and gon,
And in swich forme endure a wowke or two.
Thanne were my brother warisshed of his wo.
Thanne moste she nedes holden hire biheste,
Or elles he shal shame hire atte leeste.

WHAT sholde I make a lenger tale of
this?
Unto his brotheres bed he comen is,
And swich confort he yaf hym for to gon
To Orliens, that he up stirte anon,
And on his wey forthward thanne is he fare,
In hope for to been lissed of his care.
Whan they were come almoost to that
citee,
But if it were a two furlong or thre,
A yong clerk romynge by hymself they mette
Which that in Latyn thriftily hem grette,

The prologe of the Marchantes Tale ✿✿

EPYNG and waylyng,
care and oother sorwe
I knowe ynogh, on
even and a morwe,
Quod the Marchant,
and so doon othere mo
That wedded been, I
trowe that it be so;
for wel I woot, it fareth
so with me.
I have a wyf, the worste that may be;
for thogh the feend to hire ycoupled were,
She wolde hym overmacche, I dar wel swere.
What sholde I yow reherce in special
Hir hye malice? She is a shrewe at al.
Ther is a long and large difference
Bitwix Grisildis grete pacience
And of my wyf the passyng crueltee.
Were I unbounden, al so moot I thee!

I wolde nevere eft comen in the snare.
We wedded men lyve in sorwe and care.
Assaye whoso wole, and he shal fynde
I seye sooth, by Seint Thomas of Ynde,
As for the moore part, I sey nat alle;
God shilde that it sholde so bifalle!
A! good sir Hoost! I have ywedded bee
Thise monthes two, and moore nat, pardee!
And yet, I trowe, he that al his lyve
Wyflees hath been, though that men wolde
him ryve
Unto the herte, ne koude in no manere
Tellen so muchel sorwe, as I now heere
Koude tellen of my wyves cursednesse!
Now, quod our Hoost, Marchant, so God
yow blesse!
Syn ye so muchel knowen of that art,
ful hertely I pray yow telle us part.
Gladly, quod he, but of myn owene soore,
for soory herte, I telle may namoore.

HEERE BIGYNNETH THE MARCHANTES TALE ✿✿

THER was dwellynge in Lumbardye
A worthy knyght, that born was of Pavye,
In which he lyved in greet prosperitee;
And sixty yeer a wyflees man was hee,
And folwed ay his bodily delyt
On wommen, theras was his appetyt,
As doon thise fooles that been seculeer.
And whan that he was passed sixty yeer,
Were it for hoolynesse or for dotage
I kan nat seye, but swich a greet corage
Hadde this knyght to been a wedded man,
That day and nyght he dooth al that he kan
Tespien where he myghte wedded be;
Preyinge oure Lord to granten him, that he
Mighte ones knowe of thilke blisful lyf
That is bitwixe an housbonde and his wyf;
And for to lyve under that hooly bond
With which that first God man and womman
bond.
Noon oother lyf, seyde he, is worth a bene;
for wedlok is so esy and so clene,

That in this world it is a paradys.
Thus seyde this olde knyght, that was so
wys.
AND certeinly, as sooth as God is kyng,
To take a wyf, it is a glorious thyng;
And namely whan a man is oold and
hoor,
Thanne is a wyf the fruyt of his tresor.
Thanne sholde he take a yong wyf and a feir,
On which he myghte engendren hym an heir,
And lede his lyf in joye and in solas;
Wheras thise bacheleres synge Allas!
Whan that they fynden any adversitee
In love, which nys but childyssh vanytee.
And trewely it sit wel to be so,
That bacheleres have often peyne and wo;
On brotel ground they buylde, & brotelnesse
They fynde, whan they wene sikernesse.
They lyve but as a bryd or as a beest,
In libertee, and under noon arreest,
Theras a wedded man in his estaat
Lyveth a lyf blisful and ordinaat,
Under the yok of mariage ybounde.
Wel may his herte in joye & blisse habounde;
for who kan be so buxom as a wyf?
Who is so trewe, and eek so ententyf
To kepe hym, syk and hool, as is his make?
for wele or wo she wole hym nat forsake.
She nys nat wery hym to love and serve,
Thogh that he lye bedrede til he sterve.
AND yet somme clerkes seyn it nys
nat so,
Of whiche he, Theofraste, is oon of
tho.
What force though Theofraste liste lye?
Ne take no wyf, quod he, for housbond-
rye,
As for to spare in houshold thy dispence;
A trewe servant dooth moore diligence
Thy good to kepe, than thyn owene wyf,

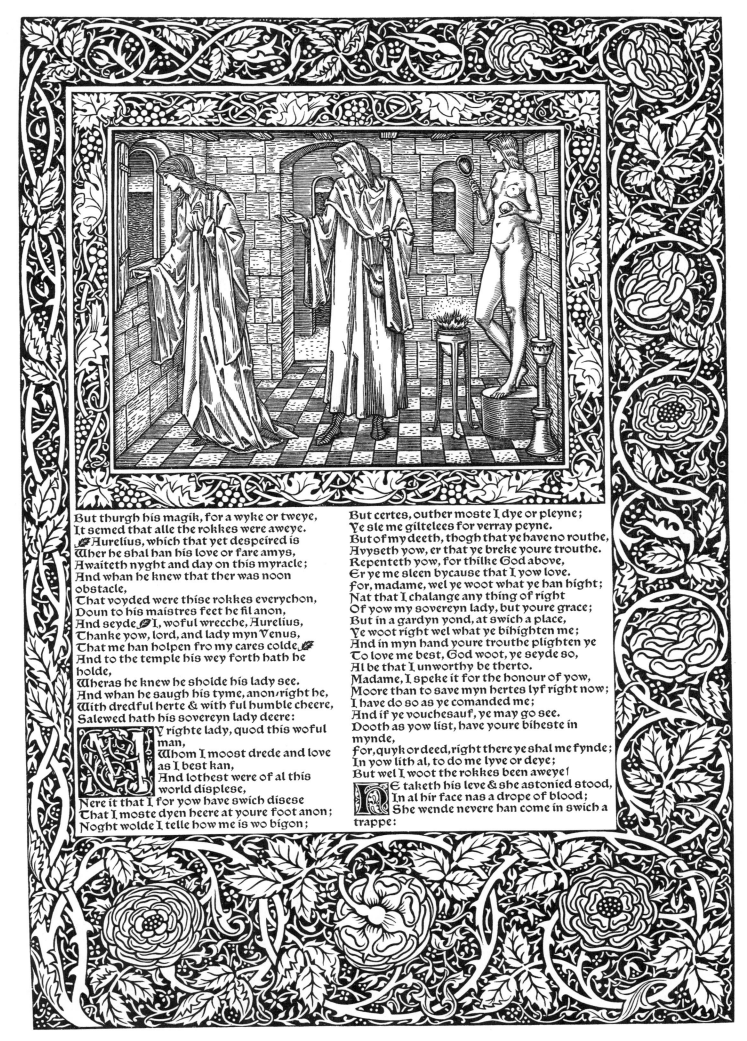

But thurgh his magik, for a wyke or tweye,
It semed that alle the rokkes were aweye.
Aurelius, which that yet despeired is
Wher he shal han his love or fare amys,
Awaiteth nyght and day on this myracle;
And whan he knew that ther was noon
    obstacle,
That voyded were thise rokkes everychon,
Doun to his maistres feet he fil anon,
And seyde I, woful wrecche, Aurelius,
Thanke yow, lord, and lady myn Venus,
That me han holpen fro my cares colde,
And to the temple his wey forth hath he
    holde,
Wheras he knew he sholde his lady see.
And whan he saugh his tyme, anon right he,
With dredful herte & with ful humble cheere,
Salewed hath his sovereyn lady deere:
MY righte lady, quod this woful
    man,
Whom I moost drede and love
    as I best kan,
And lothest were of al this
    world displese,
Nere it that I for yow have swich disese
That I moste dyen heere at youre foot anon;
Noght wolde I telle how me is wo bigon;

But certes, outher moste I dye or pleyne;
Ye sle me giltelees for verray peyne.
But of my deeth, thogh that ye have no routhe,
Avyseth yow, er that ye breke youre trouthe.
Repenteth yow, for thilke God above,
Er ye me sleen bycause that I yow love.
For, madame, wel ye woot what ye han hight;
Nat that I chalange any thing of right
Of yow my sovereyn lady, but youre grace;
But in a gardyn yond, at swich a place,
Ye woot right wel what ye bihighten me;
And in myn hand youre trouthe plighten ye
To love me best, God woot, ye seyde so,
Al be that I unworthy be therto.
Madame, I speke it for the honour of yow,
Moore than to save myn hertes lyf right now;
I have do so as ye comanded me;
And if ye vouchesauf, ye may go see.
Dooth as yow list, have youre biheste in
    mynde,
For, quyk or deed, right there ye shal me fynde;
In yow lith al, to do me lyve or deye;
But wel I woot the rokkes been aweye!
HE taketh his leve & she astonied stood,
In al hir face nas a drope of blood;
She wende nevere han come in swich a
trappe:

In swich a gyse as I shal to yow seyn
Bitwixe yow and me, and that ful soone.
Ride when yow list, ther is namoore to doone.
ENFORMED when the kyng was of
  that knyght,
  And hath conceyved in his wit aright
The manere and the forme of al this thyng,
ful glad and blithe, this noble doughty kyng
Repeireth to his revel as biforn.

THE brydel is unto the tour yborn
  And kept among his jueles leeve and
  deere,
The hors vanysshed, I noot in what manere,
Out of hir sighte; ye gete namoore of me;
But thus I lete in lust and jolitee
This Cambynskan his lordes festeyinge,
Til that wel ny the day bigan to sprynge.
Explicit prima pars. Sequitur pars secunda.

THE

NORICE OF DIGESTIOUN, the sleepe,
Gan on hem wynke, & bad hem taken keepe,
That muchel drynke & labour wolde han reste;
And with a galpyng mouth hem alle he keste,
And seyde, it was tyme to lye adoun,
for blood was in his domynacioun.
  Cherisseth blood, natures freend, quod
he
They thanken hym galpynge, by two, by thre,
And every wight gan drawe hym to his reste
As sleep hem bad; they tooke it for the beste.
HIRE dremes shal nat been ytoold for
  me;
  ful were hire heddes of fumositee,
That causeth dreem, of which ther nys no
charge.
They slepen til that it was pryme large,
The mooste part, but it were Canacee.

*Allas! quod she, that evere I was born!
Thus have I seyd, quod she, thus have I sworn,*
And toold hym al as ye han herd bifore;
It nedeth nat reherce it yow namoore.
This housbonde, with glad chiere, in freendly wyse,
Answerde and seyde as I shal yow devyse:
*Is ther oght elles, Dorigen, but this?
Nay, nay, quod she, God help me so, as wys!*
This is to muche, and it were Goddes wille.
Ye, wyf, quod he, lat sleepen that is stille;
It may be wel, paraventure, yet today.
Ye shul youre trouthe holden, by my fay!
for God so wisly have mercy upon me,
I hadde wel levere ystiked for to be,
for verray love which that I to yow have,
But if ye sholde youre trouthe kepe and save!
Trouthe is the hyeste thyng that man may kepe:

BUT with that word he brast anon to wepe,
And seyde, I yow forbede, up peyne of deeth,
That nevere, whil thee lasteth lyf ne breeth,
To no wight tel thou of this aventure.

As I may best, I wol my wo endure,
Ne make no contenance of hevynesse,
That folk of yow may demen harm or gesse.
AND forth he cleped a squier & a mayde:
Gooth forth anon with Dorigen, he sayde,
And bryngeth hire to swich a place anon.
They take hir leve, and on hir wey they gon;
But they ne wiste why she thider wente.
He nolde no wight tellen his entente.
PARAVENTURE an heep of yow, ywis,
Wol holden hym a lewed man in this,
That he wol putte his wyf in jupartie;
Herkneth the tale, er ye upon hir crie.
She may have bettre fortune than yow semeth;
And whan that ye han herd the tale, demeth.
THIS squier, which that highte Aurelius,
On Dorigen that was so amorous,
Of aventure happed hire to meete
Amydde the toun, right in the quykkest strete,
As she was bown to goon the wey forthright
Toward the gardyn theras she had hight;
And he was to the gardynward also;
for wel he spyed, whan she wolde go
Out of hir hous to any maner place.

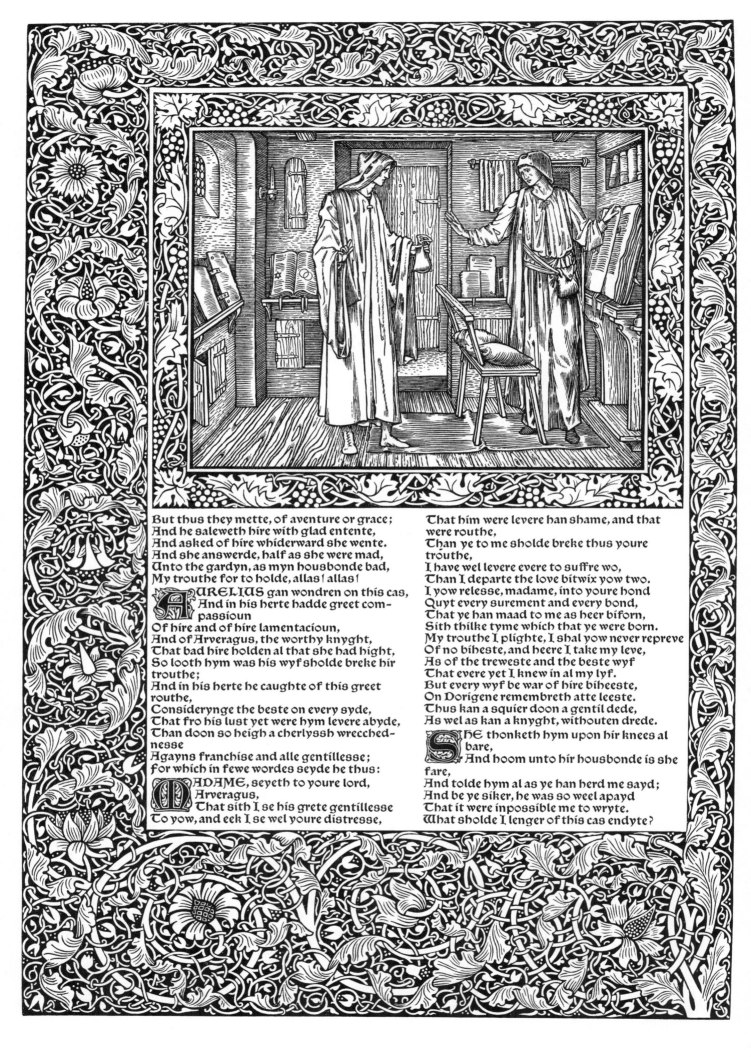

But thus they mette, of aventure or grace;
And he saleweth hire with glad entente,
And asked of hire whiderward she wente.
And she answerde, half as she were mad,
Unto the gardyn, as myn housbonde bad,
My trouthe for to holde, allas! allas!

AURELIUS gan wondren on this cas,
And in his herte hadde greet com-
passioun
Of hire and of hire lamentacioun,
And of Arveragus, the worthy knyght,
That bad hire holden al that she had hight,
So looth hym was his wyf sholde breke hir
trouthe;
And in his herte he caughte of this greet
routhe,
Considerynge the beste on every syde,
That fro his lust yet were hym levere abyde,
Than doon so heigh a cherlyssh wrecched-
nesse
Agayns franchise and alle gentillesse;
For which in fewe wordes seyde he thus:

MADAME, seyeth to youre lord,
Arveragus,
That sith I se his grete gentillesse
To yow, and eek I se wel youre distresse,

That him were levere han shame, and that
were routhe,
Than ye to me sholde breke thus youre
trouthe,
I have wel levere evere to suffre wo,
Than I departe the love bitwix yow two.
I yow relesse, madame, into youre hond
Quyt every surement and every bond,
That ye han maad to me as heer biforn,
Sith thilke tyme which that ye were born.
My trouthe I plighte, I shal yow never repreve
Of no biheste, and heere I take my leve,
As of the treweste and the beste wyf
That evere yet I knew in al my lyf.
But every wyf be war of hire biheeste,
On Dorigene remembreth atte leeste.
Thus kan a squier doon a gentil dede,
As wel as kan a knyght, withouten drede.

SHE thonketh hym upon hir knees al
bare,
And hoom unto hir housbonde is she
fare,
And tolde hym al as ye han herd me sayd;
And be ye siker, he was so weel apayd
That it were inpossible me to wryte.
What sholde I lenger of this cas endyte?

Hir nose snorted up for tene.
ful hidous was she for to sene,
ful foul and rusty was she, this.
Hir heed ywrithen was, ywis,
ful grimly with a greet towayle.

AN image of another entayle, *Felonye*
A lift half, was hir faste by;
Hir name above hir heed saugh I,
And she was called Felonye.

ANOTHER image, that Vilanye *Vilanye*
Ycleped was, saugh I and fond
Upon the walle on hir right hond.
Vilanye was lyk somdel
That other image; and, trusteth wel,
She semed a wikked creature.
By countenaunce, in portrayture,
She semed be ful despitous,
And eek ful proud and outrageous.
Wel coude he peynte, I undertake,
That swiche image coude make.
ful foul and cherlish semed she,
And eek vilaynous for to be,
And litel coude of norture,
To worshipe any creature. *Coveityse*

AND next was peynted Coveityse,
That eggeth folk, in many gyse,
To take and yeve right nought ageyn,

And grete tresours up to leyn.
And that is she that for usure
Leneth to many a creature
The lasse for the more winning,
So coveitous is her brenning.
And that is she, for penyes fele,
That techeth for to robbe and stele
These theves, and these smale harlotes;
And that is routhe, for by hir throtes
ful many oon hangeth at the laste.
She maketh folk compasse and caste
To taken other folkes thing,
Through robberie, or miscounting.
And that is she that maketh trechoures;
And she that maketh false pledoures,
That with hir termes and hir domes
Doon maydens, children, and eek gromes
Hir heritage to forgo.
ful croked were hir hondes two;
for Coveityse is ever wood
To grypen other folkes good.
Coveityse, for hir winning,
ful leef hath other mennes thing.

ANOTHER image set saugh I
Next Coveityse faste by,
And she was cleped Avarice. *Avarice*
ful foul in peynting was that vice;

Here taketh the makere of this book his leve.

NOW preye I to hem alle that herkne this litel tretys or rede, that if ther be any-thyng in it that liketh hem, that therof they thanken oure Lord Jhesu Crist, of whom procedeth al wit and al goodnesse. And if ther be anythyng that displese hem, I preye hem also that they arrette it to the defaute of myn unkonnynge, and nat to my wyl, that wolde ful fayn have seyd bettre if I hadde had konnynge. For oure boke seith: Al that is writen is writen for oure doctrine, and that is myn entente. Wher-fore I biseke yow mekely, for the mercy of God, that ye preye for me, that Crist have mercy on me & foryeve me my giltes: and namely, of my translaciouns and en-ditynges of worldly vanitees, the whiche I revoke in my retracciouns: as is The book of Troylus; The book also of Fame; The book of the Nynetene Ladies; The book of the Duchesse; The book of Seint Valen-tynes day of the Parlement of Briddes; The Tales of Caunterbury, thilke that sownen into synne; The book of the Leoun; and many another book, if they were in my remembrance; and many a song, and many a leccherous lay; that Crist, for his grete mercy, foryeve me the synne. But of the translacioun of Boece de Consolacione, & othere bookes of Legendes of Seintes, and omelies, and moralitee, & devocioun, that thanke I oure Lord Jhesu Crist and his blisful mooder, & alle the seintes of hevene; bisekynge hem that they from hennes-forth, unto my lyves ende, sende me grace to biwayle my giltes, & to studie to the sal-vacioun of my soule: and graunte me grace of verray penitence, confessioun and satis-faccioun to doon in this present lyf; thurgh the benigne grace of hym that is kyng of kynges, and preest over alle preestes, that boghte us with the precious blood of his herte; so that I may been oon of hem at the day of doome that shulle be saved. Qui cum Patre et Spiritu Sancto vivis et regnas Deus per omnia secula. Amen.

Heere is ended the book of the Tales of Caunterbury, compiled by Geffrey Chau-cer, of whos soule Jhesu Crist have mercy. Amen.

AN A.B.C. OF GEOFFREY CHAUCER

Incipit carmen secundum ordinem literarum Alphabeti.

AND AL MERCIABLE QUENE,
To whom that al this world fleeth for socour,
To have relees of sinne, sorwe and tene,
Glorious virgine, of alle floures flour,
To thee I flee, confounded in errour!
Help and releve, thou mighty debonaire,
Have mercy on my perilous langour!
Venquisshed me hath my cruel adversaire.

BOUNTEE so fix hath in thyn herte his tente,
That wel I wot thou wolt my socour be,
Thou canst not warne him that, with good entente,
Axeth thyn help. Thyn herte is ay so free,
Thou art largesse of pleyn felicitee,
Haven of refut, of quiete and of reste.
Lo, how that theves seven chasen me!
Help, lady bright, er that my ship to breste!

COMFORT is noon, but in yow, lady dere,
For lo, my sinne and my confusioun,
Which oughten not in thy presence appere,
Han take on me a grevous accioun
Of verrey right and desperacioun;
And, as by right, they mighten wel sustene
That I were worthy my dampnacioun,
Nere mercy of you, blisful hevene quene.

And of your grace granteth me som drope;
For elles may me laste ne blis ne hope,
Ne dwellen in my trouble careful herte.

WOMANLY NOBLESSE.
Balade that Chaucier made.

O hath my herte caught
in rémembraunce
Your beautè hool, and
stedfast governaunce,
Your vertues allè, and
your hy noblesse,
That you to serve is set
al my plesaunce;
So wel me lykth your
womanly contenaunce,
Your fresshe fetures and your comlinesse,
That, whyl I live, my herte to his maistresse
You hath ful chose, in trew perséveraunce,
Never to chaunge, for no maner distresse.

And sith I you shal do this observaunce
Al my lyf, withouten displesaunce,
You for to serve with al my besinesse,
Taketh me, lady, in your obeisaunce,
And have me somwhat in your souvenaunce.
My woful herte suffreth greet duresse;
And loke how humblely, with al simplesse,
My wil I cónforme to your ordenaunce,
As you best list, my peynes to redresse.

Considring eek how I hange in balaunce
In your servysè; swich, losf is my chaunce,
Abyding grace, whan that your gentilnesse
Of my gret wo list doon allegeaunce,
And with your pitè me som wyse avaunce,
In ful rebating of my hevinesse;
And thinkth, by reson, wommanly noblesse
Shuld nat desyre for to doon outrance
Theras she findeth noon unbuxumnesse.

Lenvoye.

AUCTOUR of norture, lady of
plesaunce,
Soveraine of beautè, flour of
wommanhede,
Take ye non hede unto myn
ignoraunce,
But this receyveth of your goodlihede,
Thinking that I have caught in rémembraunce
Your beautè hool, your stedfast governaunce.

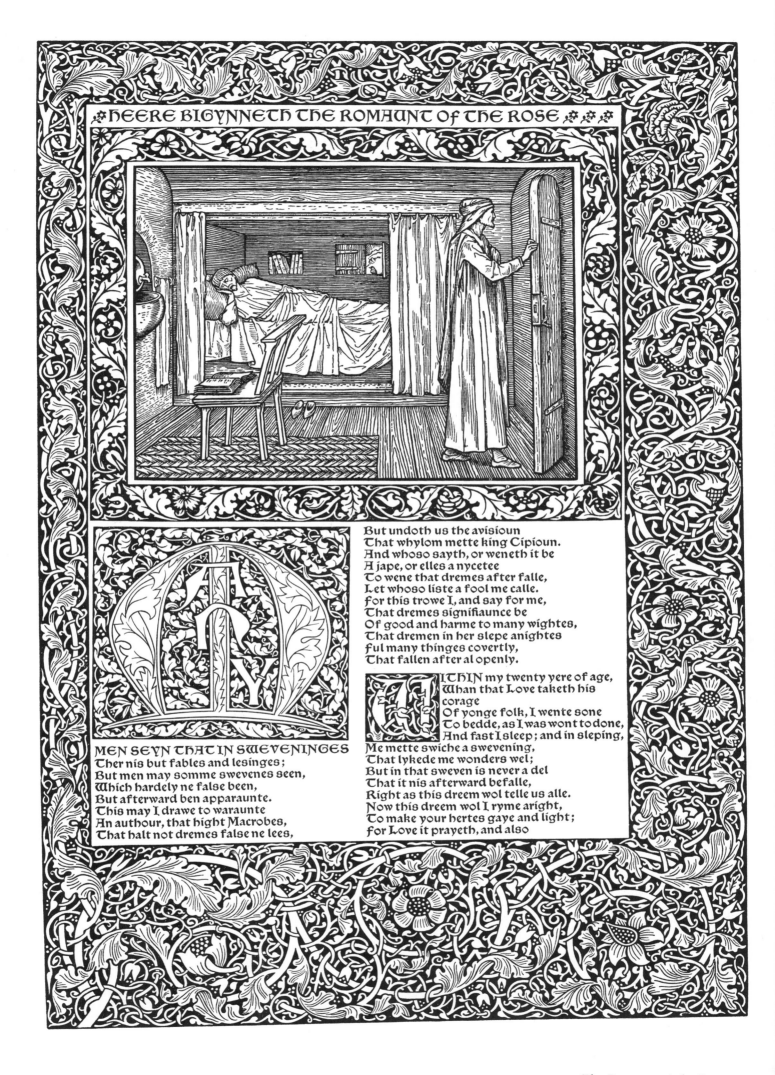

MEN SEYN THAT IN SWEVENINGES
Ther nis but fables and lesinges;
But men may somme swevenes seen,
Which hardely ne false been,
But afterward ben apparaunte.
This may I drawe to waraunte
An authour, that hight Macrobes,
That halt not dremes false ne lees,

But undoth us the avisioun
That whylom mette king Cipioun.
And whoso sayth, or weneth it be
A jape, or elles a nycetee
To wene that dremes after falle,
Let whoso liste a fool me calle.
for this trowe I, and say for me,
That dremes signifiaunce be
Of good and harme to many wightes,
That dremen in her slepe anightes
ful many thinges covertly,
That fallen after al openly.

WITHIN my twenty yere of age,
Whan that Love taketh his
corage
Of yonge folk, I wente sone
To bedde, as I was wont to done,
And fast I sleep; and in sleping,
Me mette swiche a swevening,
That lykede me wonders wel;
But in that sweven is never a del
That it nis afterward befalle,
Right as this dreem wol telle us alle.
Now this dreem wol I ryme aright,
To make your hertes gaye and light;
for Love it prayeth, and also

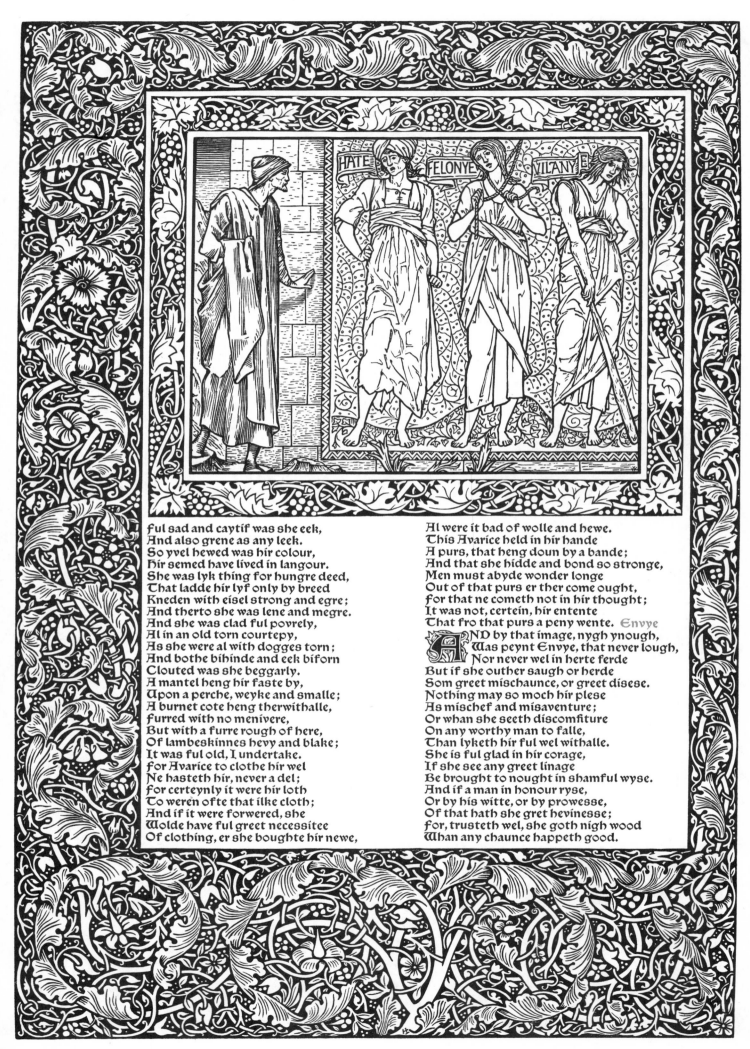

ful sad and caytif was she eek,
And also grene as any leek.
So yvel hewed was hir colour,
Hir semed have lived in langour.
She was lyk thing for hungre deed,
That ladde hir lyf only by breed
Kneden with eisel strong and egre;
And therto she was lene and megre.
And she was clad ful povrely,
Al in an old torn courtepy,
As she were al with dogges torn;
And bothe bihinde and eek biforn
Clouted was she beggarly.
A mantel heng hir faste by,
Upon a perche, weyke and smalle;
A burnet cote heng therwithalle,
Furred with no menivere,
But with a furre rough of here,
Of lambeskinnes hevy and blake;
It was ful old, I undertake.
For Avarice to clothe hir wel
Ne hasteth hir, never a del;
For certeynly it were hir loth
To weren ofte that ilke cloth;
And if it were forwered, she
Wolde have ful greet necessitee
Of clothing, er she boughte hir newe,

Al were it bad of wolle and hewe.
This Avarice held in hir hande
A purs, that heng doun by a bande;
And that she hidde and bond so stronge,
Men must abyde wonder longe
Out of that purs er ther come ought,
For that ne cometh not in hir thought;
It was not, certein, hir entente
That fro that purs a peny wente. Envye
AND by that image, nygh ynough,
Was peynt Envye, that never lough,
Nor never wel in herte ferde
But if she outher saugh or herde
Som greet mischaunce, or greet disese.
Nothing may so moch hir plese
As mischef and misaventure;
Or whan she seeth discomfiture
On any worthy man to falle,
Than lyketh hir ful wel withalle.
She is ful glad in hir corage,
If she see any greet linage
Be brought to nought in shamful wyse.
And if a man in honour ryse,
Or by his witte, or by prowesse,
Of that hath she gret hevinesse;
For, trusteth wel, she goth nigh wood
Whan any chaunce happeth good.

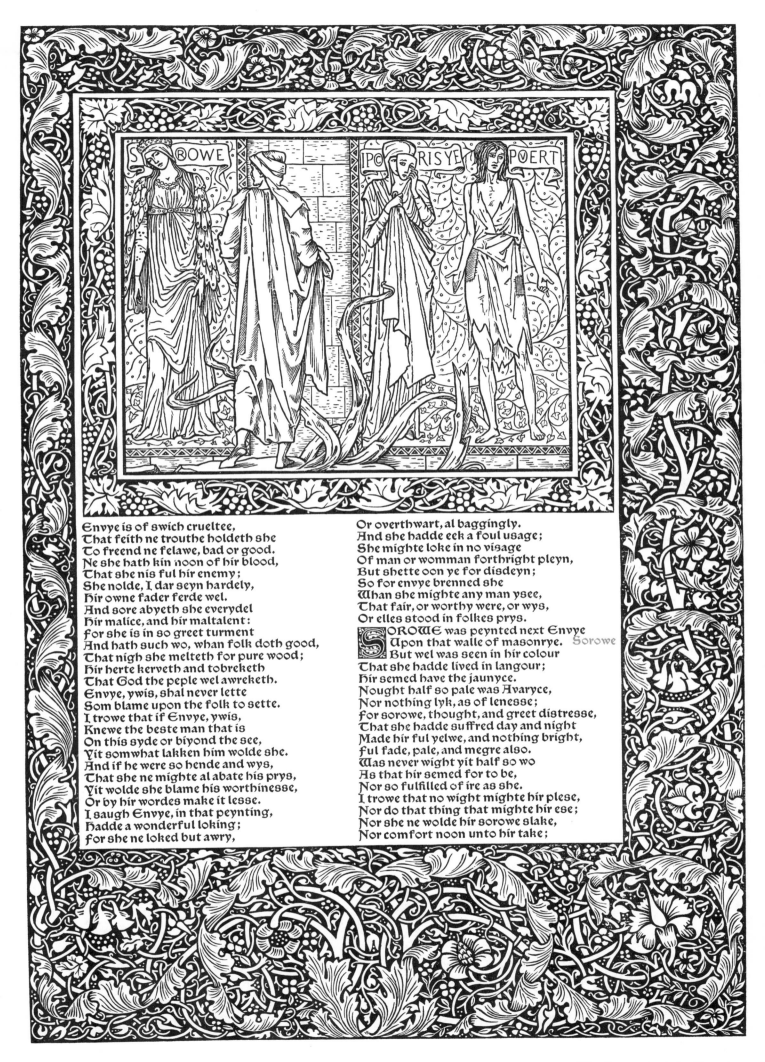

Envye is of swich crueltee,
That feith ne trouthe holdeth she
To freend ne felawe, bad or good.
Ne she hath kin noon of hir blood,
That she nis ful hir enemy;
She nolde, I dar seyn hardely,
Hir owne fader ferde wel.
And sore abyeth she everydel
Hir malice, and hir maltalent:
For she is in so greet turment
And hath such wo, whan folk doth good,
That nigh she melteth for pure wood;
Hir herte kerveth and tobreketh
That God the peple wel awreketh.
Envye, ywis, shal never lette
Som blame upon the folk to sette.
I trowe that if Envye, ywis,
Knewe the beste man that is
On this syde or biyond the see,
Yit somwhat lakken him wolde she.
And if he were so hende and wys,
That she ne mighte al abate his prys,
Yit wolde she blame his worthinesse,
Or by hir wordes make it lesse.
I saugh Envye, in that peynting,
Hadde a wonderful loking;
For she ne loked but awry,

Or overthwart, al baggingly.
And she hadde eek a foul usage;
She mighte loke in no visage
Of man or womman forthright pleyn,
But shette oon ye for disdeyn;
So for envye brenned she
Whan she mighte any man ysee,
That fair, or worthy were, or wys,
Or elles stood in folkes prys.
SOROWE was peynted next Envye
Upon that walle of masonrye. Sorowe
But wel was seen in hir colour
That she hadde lived in langour;
Hir semed have the jaunyce.
Nought half so pale was Avaryce,
Nor nothing lyk, as of lenesse;
For sorowe, thought, and greet distresse,
That she hadde suffred day and night
Made hir ful yelwe, and nothing bright,
Ful fade, pale, and megre also.
Was never wight yit half so wo
As that hir semed for to be,
Nor so fulfilled of ire as she.
I trowe that no wight mighte hir plese,
Nor do that thing that mighte hir ese;
Nor she ne wolde hir sorowe slake,
Nor comfort noon unto hir take;

And over-al diapred and writen
With ladies and with bacheleres,
Ful lightsom and ful glad of cheres.
These bowes two held Swete-Loking,
That semed lyk no gadeling.
And ten brode arowes held he there,
Of which five in his right hond were.
But they were shaven wel and dight,
Nokked and fethered aright;
And al they were with gold bigoon,
And stronge poynted everichoon,
And sharpe for to kerven weel.
But iren was ther noon ne steel;
For al was gold, men mighte it see,
Out-take the fetheres and the tree.

THE swiftest of these arowes fyve
Out of a bowe for to dryve,
And best yfethered for to flee,
And fairest eek, was cleped Beautee. Beautee
That other arowe, that hurteth lesse,
Was cleped, as I trowe, Simplesse. Simplesse
The thridde cleped was Fraunchyse, Fraun-
That fethered was, in noble wyse,   chyse
With valour and with curtesye.
The fourthe was cleped Companye, Com-
That hevy for to sheten is;   panye
But whoso sheteth right, ywis,

May therwith doon gret harm and wo.
The fifte of these, and laste also,
Fair-Semblaunt men that arowe calle,   Fair-
The leeste grevous of hem alle;   Semblaunt
Yit can it make a ful gret wounde,
But he may hope his sores sounde,
That hurt is with that arowe, ywis;
His wo the bet bistowed is.
For he may soner have gladnesse,
His langour oughte be the lesse.

FYVE arowes were of other gyse,
That been ful foule to devyse;
For shaft and ende, sooth to telle,
Were al so black as feend in helle.

THE first of hem is called Pryde; Pryde
That other arowe next him bisyde,
It was ycleped Vilanye;   Vilanye
That arowe was as with felonye
Envenimed, and with spitous blame.
The thridde of hem was cleped Shame. Shame
The fourthe, Wanhope cleped is,   Wanhope
The fifte, the Newe-Thought, ywis.   Newe-
THESE arowes that I speke   Thought
of here,
Were alle fyve of oon manere,
And alle were they resemblable.
To hem was wel sitting and able

The foule croked bowe hidous,
That knotty was, and al roynous.
That bowe semede wel to shete
These arowes fyve, that been unmete,
Contrarie to that other fyve.
But though I telle not as blyve
Of hir power, ne of hir might,
Herafter shal I tellen right
The sothe, and eek signifiaunce,
As fer as I have remembraunce:
Al shal be seid, I undertake,
Er of this boke an ende I make.

OW come I to my tale ageyn.
But alderfirst, I wol you seyn
The fasoun and the counten-
aunces
Of al the folk that on the
daunce is.
The God of Love, jolyf and light,
Ladde on his honde a lady bright,
Of high prys, and of greet degree.
This lady called was Beautee,
As was an arowe, of which I tolde.
Ful wel ythewed was she holde;
Ne she was derk ne broun, but bright,
And cleer as is the monelight,
Ageyn whom alle the sterres semen
But smale candels, as we demen.

Hir flesh was tendre as dewe of flour,
Hir chere was simple as byrde in bour;
As whyt as lilie or rose in rys,
Hir face gentil and tretys.
Fetys she was, and smal to see;
No windred browes hadde she,
Ne popped hir, for it neded nought
To windre hir, or to peynte hir ought.
Hir tresses yelowe and longe straughten,
Unto hir heles doun they raughten:
Hir nose, hir mouth, and eye and cheke
Wel wrought, and al the remenaunt eke.
A ful grete savour and a swote
Me thinketh in myn herte rote,
As helpe me God, whan I remembre
Of the fasoun of every membre!
In world is noon so fair a wight;
For yong she was, and hewed bright,
Sadde, plesaunt, and fetys withalle,
Gente, and in hir middel smalle. Richesse

ISYDE Beaute yede Richesse,
An high lady of greet noblesse,
And greet of prys in every place.
But whoso durste to hir
trespace,
Or til hir folk, in worde or dede,
He were ful hardy, out of drede;
For bothe she helpe and hindre may:

Have litel thought but on hir play.
Hir lemman was bisyde alway,
In swich a gyse, that he hir kiste
At alle tymes that him liste,
That al the daunce mighte it see;
They make no force of privetee;
for who spak of hem yvel or wel,
They were ashamed never a del,
But men mighte seen hem kisse there,
As it two yonge douves were.
for yong was thilke bachelere,
Of beaute wot I noon his pere;
And he was right of swich an age
As Youthe his leef, and swich corage.

THE lusty folk thus daunced there,
And also other that with hem were,
That weren alle of hir meynee;
ful hende folk, and wys, and free,
And folk of fair port, trewely,
Ther weren alle comunly.

WHAN I hadde seen the counte-
naunces
Of hem that ladden thus these
daunces,
Than hadde I wil to goon & see
The gardin that so lyked me,
And loken on these faire loreres,
On pyn-trees, cedres, and oliveres.

The daunces than y-ended were;
for many of hem that daunced there
Were with hir loves went awey
Under the trees to have hir pley.

A, lord! they lived lustily!
A gret fool were he, sikerly,
That nolde, his thankes, swich lyf
lede!
for this dar I seyn, out of drede,
That whoso mighte so wel fare,
for better lyf thurte him not care;
for ther nis so good paradys
As have a love at his devys.

OUT of that place wente I tho,
And in that gardin gan I go,
Pleying along ful merily.
The God of Love ful hastely
Unto him Swete-Loking clepte,
No lenger wolde he that he kepte
His bowe of golde, that shoon so bright.
He bad him bende it anon-right;
And he ful sone it sette on ende,
And at a braid he gan it bende,
And took him of his arowes fyve,
ful sharpe and redy for to dryve.
Now God that sit in magestee
fro deedly woundes kepe me,
If so be that he wol me shete;

for if I with his arowe mete,
It wol me greven sore, ywis!
But I, that nothing wiste of this,
Wente up and doun ful many a wey,
And he me folwed faste alwey;
But nowher wolde I reste me,
Til I hadde al the yerde in be.
THE gardin was, by mesuring,
Right even and squar in compassing;
It was as long as it was large.
Of fruyt had every tree his charge,
But it were any hidous tree   The Trees
Of which ther were two or three.
Ther were, and that wot I ful wel,
Of pomgarnettes a ful gret del;
That is a fruyt ful wel to lyke,
Namely to folk whan they ben syke.
And trees ther were, greet foisoun,
That baren notes in hir sesoun,
Such as men notemigges calle,
That swote of savour been withalle.
And alemandres greet plentee,
figes, and many a date-tree
Ther weren, if men hadde nede,
Through the gardin in length and brede.
Ther was eek wexing many a spyce,
As clow-gelofre, and licoryce,
Gingere, and greyn de paradys,

Canelle, and setewale of prys,
And many a spyce delitable,
To eten whan men ryse fro table.
And many hoomly trees ther were,
That peches, coynes, and apples bere,
Medlers, ploumes, peres, chesteynes,
Cheryse, of whiche many on fayn is,
Notes, aleys, and bolas,
That for to seen it was solas;
With many high lorer and pyn
Was renged clene al that gardyn;
With cipres, and with oliveres,
Of which that nigh no plente here is.
Ther were elmes grete and stronge,
Maples, asshe, ook, asp, planes longe,
fyn ew, popler, and lindes faire,
And other trees ful many a payre.
WHAT sholde I telle you more of it?
Ther were so many trees yit,
That I sholde al encombred be
Er I had rekened every tree.
THESE trees were set, that I devyse,
Oon from another, in assyse,
five fadome or sixe, I trowe so,
But they were hye and grete also:
And for to kepe out wel the sonne,
The croppes were so thikke yronne,
And every braunch in other knet,

Wel semed by hir apparayle
She was not wont to greet travayle.
For whan she kempt was fetisly,
And wel arayed and richely,
Thanne had she doon al hir journee;
For mery and wel bigoon was she.
She ladde a lusty lyf in May,
She hadde no thought, by night ne day,
Of nothing, but it were oonly
To graythe hir wel and uncouthly.

WHAN that this dore hadde opened me
This mayden, semely for to see,
I thanked hir as I best mighte,
And axede hir how that she highte,
And what she was, I axede eke.
And she to me was nought unmeke,
Ne of hir answer daungerous,
But faire answerde, and seide thus:

LO, sir, my name is Ydelnesse;
So clepe men me, more & lesse.
Ful mighty and ful riche am I,
And that of oon thing, namely;
For I entende to nothing
But to my joye, and my pleying,
And for to kembe and tresse me.
Aqueynted am I, and privee
With Mirthe, lord of this gardyn,

That fro the lande of Alexandryn
Made the trees be hider fet,
That in this gardin been yset.
And whan the trees were woxen on highte,
This wal, that stant here in thy sighte,
Dide Mirthe enclosen al aboute;
And these images, al withoute,
He dide hem bothe entaile and peynte,
That neither ben jolyf ne queynte,
But they ben ful of sorowe and wo,
As thou hast seen a whyle ago.

AND ofte tyme, him to solace,
Sir Mirthe cometh into this place,
And eek with him cometh his meynee,
That liven in lust and jolitee.
And now is Mirthe therin, to here
The briddes, how they singen clere,
The mavis and the nightingale,
And other joly briddes smale.
And thus he walketh to solace
Him and his folk; for swetter place
To pleyen in he may not finde,
Although he soughte oon intil Inde.
The altherfairest folk to see
That in this world may founde be
Hath Mirthe with him in his route,
That folowen him alwayes aboute.

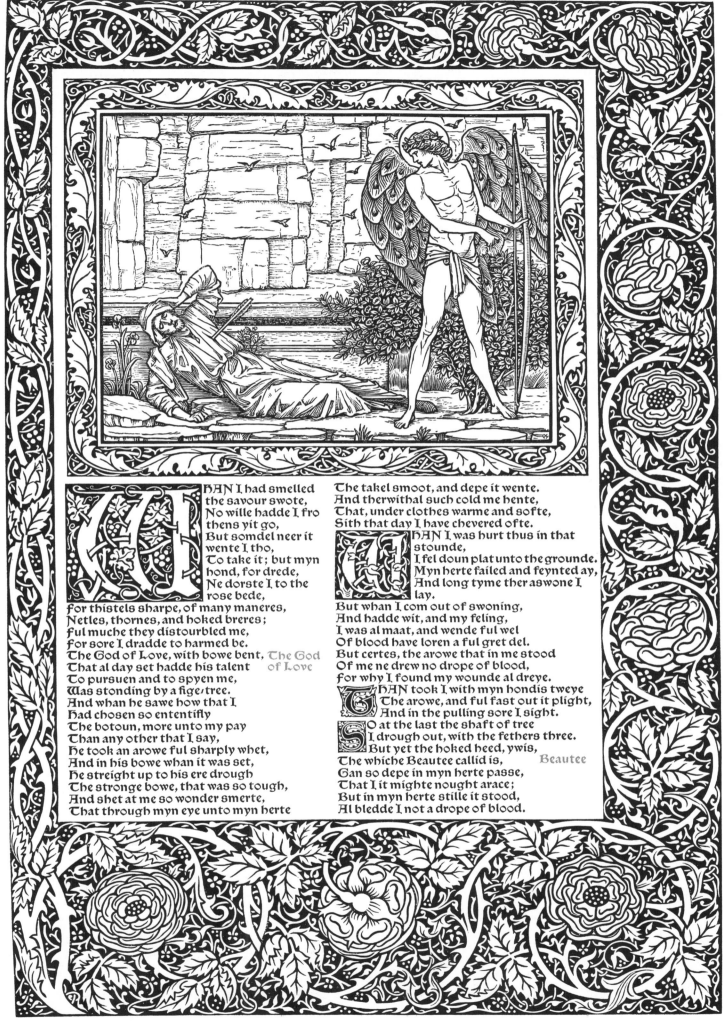

WHAN I had smelled the savour swote, No wille hadde I fro thens yit go, But somdel neer it wente I tho, To take it; but myn hond, for drede, Ne dorste I to the rose bede, for thistels sharpe, of many maneres, Netles, thornes, and hoked breres; ful muche they distourbled me, for sore I dradde to harmed be. The God of Love, with bowe bent, That al day set hadde his talent To pursuen and to spyen me, Was stonding by a fige-tree. And whan he sawe how that I Had chosen so ententifly The botoun, more unto my pay Than any other that I say, He took an arowe ful sharply whet, And in his bowe whan it was set, He streight up to his ere drough The stronge bowe, that was so tough, And shet at me so wonder smerte, That through myn eye unto myn herte

The God of Love

The takel smoot, and depe it wente. And therwithal such cold me hente, That, under clothes warme and softe, Sith that day I have chevered ofte. WHAN I was hurt thus in that stounde, I fel doun plat unto the grounde. Myn herte failed and feynted ay, And long tyme ther aswone I lay. But whan I com out of swoning, And hadde wit, and my feling, I was al maat, and wende ful wel Of blood have loren a ful gret del. But certes, the arowe that in me stood Of me ne drew no drope of blood, for why I found my wounde al dreye. THAN took I with myn hondis tweye The arowe, and ful fast out it plight, And in the pulling sore I sight. So at the last the shaft of tree I drough out, with the fethers three. But yet the hoked heed, ywis, The whiche Beautee callid is, Gan so depe in myn herte passe, That I it mighte nought arace; But in myn herte stille it stood, Al bledde I not a drope of blood.

Beautee

She was nought rude ne unmete,
But couthe ynow of swich doing
As longeth unto caroling:
For she was wont in every place
To singen first, folk to solace;
For singing most she gaf hir to;
No craft had she so leef to do.
THO mightest thou caroles seen,
And folk ther daunce and mery been,
And make many a fair tourning
Upon the grene gras springing.
Ther mightest thou see these floutours,
Minstrales, and eek jogelours,
That wel to singe dide hir peyne.
Somme songe songes of Loreyne;
For in Loreyne hir notes be
Ful swetter than in this contree.
Ther was many a timbestere,
And saylours, that I dar wel swere
Couthe hir craft ful parfitly.
The timbres up ful sotilly
They caste, and henten hem ful ofte
Upon a finger faire and softe,
That they ne fayled nevermo.
Ful fetis damiselles two,
Right yonge, and fulle of semlihede,
In kirtles, and non other wede,
And faire tressed every tresse,

Hadde Mirthe doon, for his noblesse,
Amidde the carole for to daunce;
But herof lyth no remembraunce,
How that they daunced queyntely.
That oon wolde come al prively
Agayn that other: and whan they were
Togidre almost, they threwe yfere
Hir mouthes so, that through hir play
It semed as they kiste alway;
To dauncen wel coude they the gyse;
What shulde I more to you devyse?
Ne bede I never thennes go,
Whyles that I saw hem daunce so. Curtesye
UPON the carole wonder faste
I gan biholde; til atte laste
A lady gan me for to espye,
And she was cleped Curtesye,
The worshipful, the debonaire;
I pray God ever falle hir faire!
Ful curteisly she called me,
What do ye there, beau sire? quod she,
Come neer, and if it lyke yow
To dauncen, daunceth with us now.
And I, withoute tarying,
Wente into the caroling.
I was abasshed never a del,
But it me lykede right wel
That Curtesye me cleped so,

HERE·STARF·THE·FAIRE·NARCISSVS

That Narcisus somtyme him bere.
He quitte him wel his guerdon there;
for he so musede in the welle,
That, shortly al the sothe to telle,
He lovede his owne shadowe so,
That atte laste he starf for wo.
for whan he saugh that he his wille
Mighte in no maner wey fulfille,
And that he was so faste caught
That he him couthe comfort naught,
He loste his wit right in that place,
And deyde within a litel space.
And thus his warisoun he took
for the lady that he forsook.
LADYES, I preye ensample taketh,
Ye that ayeins your love mistaketh:
for if hir deeth be yow to wyte,
God can ful wel your whyle quyte.
WHAN that this lettre, of whiche
I telle,
Had taught me that it was the
welle
Of Narcisus in his beautee,
I gan anoon withdrawe me,
Whan it fel in my remembraunce,
That him bitidde swich mischaunce.
But at the laste than thoughte I,
That scatheles, ful sikerly,

I mighte unto The Welle go.
Wherof shulde I abasshen so?
Unto the welle than wente I me,
And doun I louted for to see
The clere water in the stoon,
And eek the gravel, which that shoon
Down in the botme, as silver fyn;
for of the welle, this is the fyn,
In world is noon so cleer of hewe.
The water is ever fresh and newe
That welmeth up with wawes brighte
The mountance of two finger highte.
Abouten it is gras springing,
for moiste so thikke and wel lyking,
That it ne may in winter dye,
No more than may the see be drye.
DOWN at the botme set saw I
Two cristal stones craftely
In thilke fresshe and faire welle.
But o thing soothly dar I telle,
That ye wol holde a greet mervayle
Whan it is told, withouten fayle.
for whan the sonne, cleer in sighte,
Cast in that welle his bemes brighte,
And that the heet descended is,
Than taketh the cristal stoon, ywis,
Agayn the sonne an hundred hewes,
Blewe, yelowe, & rede, that fresh and newe is.

The Welle

for curteys, and of fair manere,
Wel taught, and ful of gentilnesse
He muste ben, that shal me kisse,
And also of ful high fraunchyse,
That shal atteyne to that empryse.
And first of o thing warne I thee,
That peyne and gret adversitee
He mot endure, and eek travaile,
That shal me serve, withoute faile,
But ther ageyns, thee to comforte,
And with thy servise to desporte,
Thou mayst ful glad and joyful be
So good a maister to have as me,
And lord of so high renoun.
I bere of Love the gonfanoun,
Of Curtesye the banere;
for I am of the silf manere,
Gentil, curteys, meek and free;
That whosoever ententif be
Me to honoure, doute, and serve,
And also that he him observe
fro trespas and fro vilanye,
And him governe in curtesye
With wil and with entencioun;
for whan he first in my prisoun
Is caught, than muste he uttirly,
fro thennesforth ful bisily,
Caste him gentil for to be,

If he desyre helpe of me.
ANOON withouten more delay,
Withouten daunger or affray,
I becom his man anoon,
And gave him thankes many a oon,
And kneled doun with hondis joynt,
And made it in my port ful queynt;
The joye went to myn herte rote.
Whan I had kissed his mouth so swote,
I had sich mirthe and sich lyking,
It cured me of languisshing.
He askid of me than hostages:
I HAVE, he seide, taken fele homages
Of oon and other, where I have been
Disceyved ofte, withouten wene.
These felouns, fulle of falsitee,
Have many sythes bigyled me,
And through falshede hir lust acheved,
Wherof I repente and am agreved.
And I hem gete in my daungere,
Hir falshed shulle they bye ful dere.
But for I love thee, I seye thee pleyn,
I wol of thee be more certeyn;
for thee so sore I wol now binde,
That thou away ne shalt not winde
for to denyen the covenaunt,
Or doon that is not avenaunt.
That thou were fals it were gret reuthe,

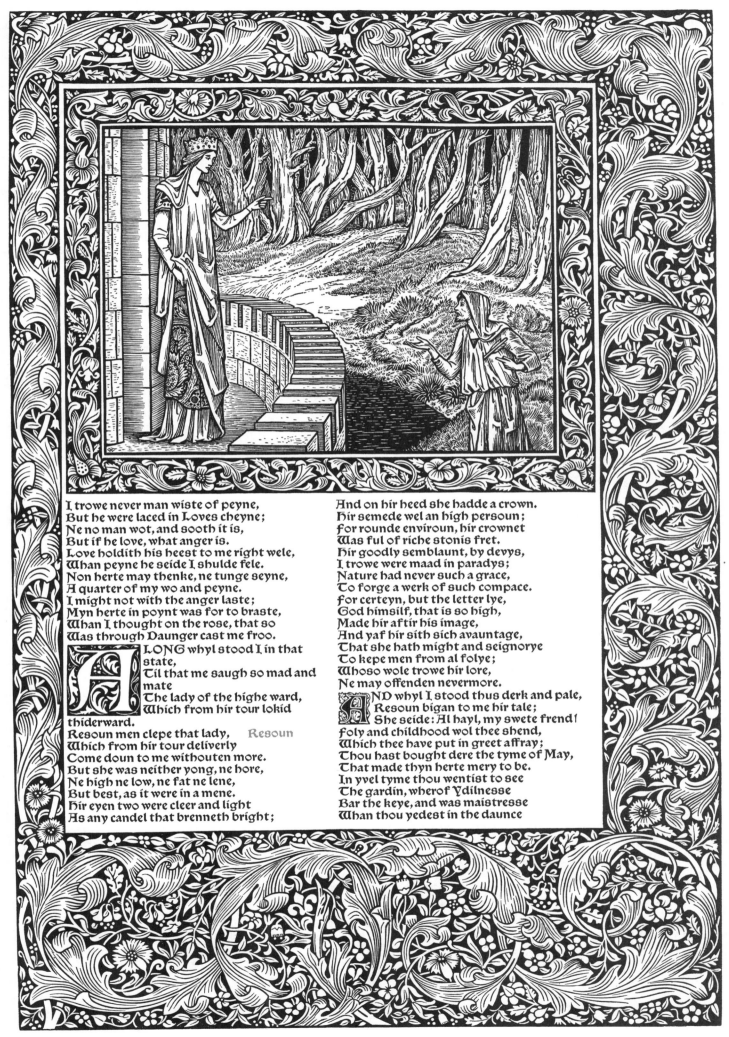

I trowe never man wiste of peyne,
But he were laced in Loves cheyne;
Ne no man wot, and sooth it is,
But if he love, what anger is.
Love holdith his heest to me right wele,
Whan peyne he seide I shulde fele.
Non herte may thenke, ne tunge seyne,
A quarter of my wo and peyne.
I might not with the anger laste;
Myn herte in poynt was for to braste,
Whan I thought on the rose, that so
Was through Daunger cast me froo.

ALONG whyl stood I in that
state,
Til that me saugh so mad and
mate
The lady of the highe ward,
Which from hir tour lokid
thiderward.
Resoun men clepe that lady,   Resoun
Which from hir tour deliverly
Come doun to me withouten more.
But she was neither yong, ne hore,
Ne high ne low, ne fat ne lene,
But best, as it were in a mene.
Hir eyen two were cleer and light
As any candel that brenneth bright;

And on hir heed she hadde a crown.
Hir semede wel an high persoun;
For rounde enviroun, hir crownet
Was ful of riche stonis fret.
Hir goodly semblaunt, by devys,
I trowe were maad in paradys;
Nature had never such a grace,
To forge a werk of such compace.
For certeyn, but the letter lye,
God himsilf, that is so high,
Made hir aftir his image,
And yaf hir sith sich avauntage,
That she hath might and seignorye
To kepe men from al folye;
Whoso wole trowe hir lore,
Ne may offenden nevermore.

AND whyl I stood thus derk and pale,
Resoun bigan to me hir tale;
She seide: Al hayl, my swete frend!
Foly and childhood wol thee shend,
Which thee have put in greet affray;
Thou hast bought dere the tyme of May,
That made thyn herte mery to be.
In yvel tyme thou wentist to see
The gardin, wherof Ydilnesse
Bar the keye, and was maistresse
Whan thou yedest in the daunce

feithful, and ful of stabilite.
Good Hope alwey kepe by thy syde,
And Swete Thought make eek abyde,
Swete Loking and Swete Speche;
Of alle thyn harmes they shal be leche.
Of every thou shalt have greet plesaunce;
If thou canst byde in sufferaunce,
And serve wel without feyntyse,
Thou shalt be quit of thyn empryse,
With more guerdoun, if that thou live;
But al this tyme this I thee yive.

THE God of Love whan al the day
Had taught me, as ye have herd say,
And enfourmed compendiously,
He vanished awey al sodeynly,
And I alone lefte, al sole,
So ful of compleynt and of dole,
For I saw no man ther me by.
My woundes me greved wondirly;
Me for to curen nothing I knew,
Save the botoun bright of hew,
Wheron was set hoolly my thought;
Of other comfort knew I nought,
But it were through the God of Love;
I knew nat elles to my bihove

That might me ese or comfort gete,
But if he wolde him entermete.

THE roser was, withoute doute,
Closed with an hegge withoute,
As ye toforn have herd me seyn;
And fast I bisied, and wolde fayn
Have passed the haye, if I might
Have geten in by any slight
Unto the botoun so fair to see.
But ever I dradde blamed to be,
If men wolde have suspeccioun
That I wolde of entencioun
Have stole the roses that ther were;
Therfore to entre I was in fere.
But at the last, as I bithought
Whether I sholde passe or nought,
I saw come with a gladde chere
To me, a lusty bachelere,
Of good stature, and of good hight,
And Bialacoil forsothe he hight.   Bialacoil
Sone he was to Curtesy,
And he me graunted ful gladly
The passage of the outer hay,
And seide: Sir, how that ye may
Passe, if it your wille be,
The fresshe roser for to see,
And ye the swete savour fele.
Your warrant may I be right wele;

So thou thee kepe fro folye,
Shal no man do thee vilanye.
If I may helpe you in ought,
I shal not feyne, dredeth nought;
for I am bounde to your servyse,
fully devoide of feyntyse.

THAN unto Bialacoil saide I:
I thank you, sir, ful hertely,
And your biheest I take at gree,
That ye so goodly profer me;
To you it cometh of greet fraunchyse,
That ye me profer your servyse.

Than aftir, ful deliverly,
Through the breres anoon wente I,
Wherof encombred was the hay.
I was wel plesed, the soth to say,
To see the botoun fair and swote,
So fresshe spronge out of the rote.
And Bialacoil me served wel,
Whan I so nygh me mighte fele
Of the botoun the swete odour,
And so lusty hewed of colour.

BUT than a cherl, foule him bityde!
Bisyde the roses gan him hyde,
To kepe the roses of that roser,
Of whom the name was Daunger.   Daunger
This cherl was hid there in the greves,
Covered with grasse and with leves,

To spye and take whom that he fond
Unto that roser putte an hond.
He was not sole, for ther was mo;
for with him were other two
Of wikkid maners, and yvel fame.   Wikked
That oon was clepid, by his name,   Tonge
Wikked-Tonge, God yeve him sorwe!
for neither at eve, ne at morwe,
He can of no man no good speke;
On many a just man doth he wreke.
Ther was a womman eek, that hight
Shame, that, who can reken right,   Shame
Trespas was hir fadir name,
Hir moder Resoun; and thus was Shame
On lyve brought of these ilk two.
And yit had Trespas never ado
With Resoun, ne never ley hir by,
He was so hidous and ugly,
I mene, this that Trespas hight;
But Resoun conceyveth, of a sight,
Shame, of that I spak aforn.   Chastitee

AND when that Shame was thus born,
It was ordeyned, that Chastitee
Shulde of the roser lady be,
Which, of the botouns more and las,
With sondry folk assailed was,
That she ne wiste what to do.
for Venus hir assailith so,

Han seid such harm and shame now,
Witeth wel, if he gessed it,
Ye may wel demen in your wit,
He nolde nothing love you so,
Ne callen you his freend also,
But night and day he wolde wake,
The castel to destroye and take,
If it were sooth as ye devyse;
Or som man in som maner wyse
Might it warne him everydel,
Or by himself perceyven wel;
For sith he might not come and gon
As he was whylom wont to don,
He might it sone wite and see;
But now al otherwyse doth he.
Than have ye, sir, al outerly
Deserved helle, and jolyly
The deth of helle, douteles,
That thrallen folk so gilteles.

FALS/SEMBLANT proveth so
this thing
That he can noon answering,
And seeth alwey such apparaunce,
That nygh he fel in repentaunce,
And seide him: Sir, it may wel be.
Semblant, a good man semen ye;
And, Abstinence, ful wyse ye seme;
Of o talent you bothe I deme.

What counceil wole ye to me yeven?
Fals/Semblant.
RIGHT here anoon thou shalt be
shriven,
And sey thy sinne withoute more;
Of this shalt thou repente sore;
For I am preest, and have poustee
To shryve folk of most dignitee
That been, as wyde as world may dure.
Of al this world I have the cure,
And that had never yit persoun,
No vicarie of no maner toun.
And, God wot, I have of thee
A thousand tymes more pitee
Than hath thy preest parochial,
Though he thy freend be special.
I have avauntage, in o wyse,
That your prelates ben not so wyse
Ne half so lettred as am I.
I am licenced boldely
In divinitee to rede,
And to confessen, out of drede.
If ye wol you now confesse,
And leve your sinnes more and lesse,
Without abood, knele doun anon,
And you shal have absolucion.

Here ends all that is done of The Romance
of the Rose.

❀❀ THE PARLEMENT OF FOULES ❀❀ THE PROEM. ❀❀❀❀

The lyf so short, the craft so long to lerne,
Thassay so hard, so sharp the conquering,
The dredful joy, that alwey slit so yerne,
Al this mene I by love, that my feling
Astonyeth with his wonderful worching
So sore ywis, that whan I on him thinke,
Nat wot I wel wher that I wake or winke.

For al be that I knowe not love in dede,
Ne wot how that he quyteth folk hir hyre,
Yet happeth me ful ofte in bokes rede
Of his miracles, and his cruel yre;
Ther rede I wel he wol be lord and syre,
I dar not seyn, his strokes been so sore,
But God save swich a lord! I can no more.

Of usage, what for luste what for lore,
On bokes rede I ofte, as I yow tolde.
But wherfor that I speke al this? not yore
Agon, hit happed me for to beholde
Upon a boke, was write with lettres olde;
And therupon, a certeyn thing to lerne,
The longe day ful faste I radde and yerne.

For out of olde feldes, as men seith,
Cometh al this newe corn fro yeer to yere;
And out of olde bokes, in good feith,
Cometh al this newe science that men lere.
But now to purpos as of this matere...
To rede forth hit gan me so delyte,
That al the day me thoughte but a lyte.

This book of which I make mencioun,
Entitled was al thus, as I shal telle,
Tullius of the dreme of Scipioun;

The olyve of pees, and eek the drunken vyne,
The victor palm, the laurer to devyne.

A garden saw I, ful of blosmy bowes,
Upon a river, in a grene mede,
Ther as that swetnesse evermore ynow is,
With floures whyte, blewe, yelowe, and rede;
And colde welle-stremes, nothing dede,
That swommen ful of smale fisshes lighte,
With finnes rede and scales silver-brighte.

On every bough the briddes herde I singe,
With voys of aungel in hir armonye,
Som besyed hem hir briddes forth to bringe;
The litel conyes to hir pley gunne hye,
And further al aboute I gan espye
The dredful roo, the buk, the hert and hinde,
Squerels, and bestes smale of gentil kinde.

Of instruments of strenges in acord
Herde I so pleye a ravisshing swetnesse,
That God, that maker is of al and lord,
Ne herde never better, as I gesse;
Therwith a wind, unnethe hit might be lesse,
Made in the leves grene a noise softe
Acordant to the foules songe on-lofte.

The air of that place so attempre was

That never was grevaunce of hoot ne cold;
Ther wex eek every holsom spyce and gras,
Ne no man may ther wexe seek ne old;
Yet was ther joye more a thousand fold
Then man can telle; ne never wolde it nighte,
But ay cleer day to any mannes sighte.

Under a tree, besyde a welle, I say
Cupyde our lord his arwes forge and fyle;
And at his fete his bowe al redy lay,
And wel his doghter tempred al the whyle
The hedes in the welle, and with hir wyle
She couched hem after as they shulde serve,
Som for to slee, and som to wounde and kerve.

Tho was I war of Plesaunce anon-right,
And of Aray, and Lust, and Curtesye;
And of the Craft that can and hath the might
To doon by force a wight to do folye,
Disfigurat was she, I nil not lye;
And by himself, under an oke, I gesse,
Sawe I Delyt, that stood with Gentilnesse.

I saw Beautee, withouten any atyr,
And Youthe, ful of game and jolyte,
Fool-hardinesse, flatery, and Desyr,
Messagerye, and Mede, and other three,
Hir names shul noght here be told-for me,

And upon pilers grete of jasper longe
I saw a temple of bras yfounded stronge.

Aboute the temple daunceden alway
Wommen ynowe, of whiche somme ther were
faire of hemself, and somme of hem were gay;
In kirtels, al disshevele, wente they there,
That was hir office alwey, yeer by yere,
And on the temple, of doves whyte and faire
Saw I sittinge many a hundred paire.

Before the temple-dore ful soberly
Dame Pees sat, with a curteyn in hir hond:
And hir besyde, wonder discretly,
Dame Pacience sitting ther I fond
With face pale, upon an hille of sond;
And alder-next, within and eek withoute,
Behest and Art, and of hir folke a route.

Within the temple, of syghes hote as fyr
I herde a swogh that gan aboute renne;
Which syghes were engendred with desyr,
That maden every auter for to brenne
Of newe flaume; and wel aspyed I thenne
That al the cause of sorwes that they drye
Com of the bitter goddesse Jalousye.

The god Priapus saw I, as I wente,

Within the temple, in soverayn place stonde,
In swich aray as whan the asse him shente
With crye by night, and with his ceptre in
honde;
ful besily men gunne assaye and fonde
Upon his hede to sette, of sondry hewe,
Garlondes ful of fresshe floures newe.

And in a privee corner, in disporte,
fond I Venus and hir porter Richesse,
That was ful noble and hauteyn of hir porte;
Derk was that place, but afterward lightnesse
I saw a lyte, unnethe hit might be lesse,
And on a bed of golde she lay to reste,
Til that the hote sonne gan to weste.

Hir gilte heres with a golden threde
Ybounden were, untressed as she lay,
And naked fro the breste unto the hede
Men might hir see; and, sothly for to say,
The remenant wel kevered to my pay
Right with a subtil kerchef of Valence,
Ther was no thikker cloth of no defence.

The place yaf a thousand savours swote,
And Bachus, god of wyn, sat hir besyde,
And Ceres next, that doth of hunger bote;
And, as I seide, amiddes lay Cipryde,

To whom on knees two yonge folkes cryde
To ben hir help; but thus I leet hir lye,
And ferther in the temple I gan espye

That, in dispyte of Diane the chaste,
Ful many a bowe ybroke heng on the wal
Of maydens, suche as gunne hir tymes waste
In hir servyse; and peynted over al
Of many a story, of which I touche shal
A fewe, as of Calixte and Athalaunte,
And many a mayde, of which the name I
wante;

Semyramus, Candace, and Ercules,
Biblis, Dido, Tisbe and Piramus,
Tristram, Isoude, Paris, and Achilles,
Eleyne, Cleopatre, and Troilus,
Silla, and eek the moder of Romulus...
Alle these were peynted on that other syde,
And al hir love, and in what plyte they dyde.

When I was come ayen into the place
That I of spak, that was so swote & greene,
Forth welk I tho, myselven to solace.
Tho was I war wher that ther sat a quene
That, as of light the somer-sonne shene
Passeth the sterre, right so over mesure
She fairer was than any creature.

And in a launde, upon an hille of floures,
Was set this noble goddesse Nature;
Of braunches were hir halles and hir boures,
Ywrought after hir craft and hir mesure;
Ne ther nas foul that cometh of engendrure,
That they ne were prest in hir presence,
To take hir doom and yeve hir audience.

For this was on seynt Valentynes day,
Whan every foul cometh ther to chese his
make,
Of every kinde, that men thenke may;
And that so huge a noyse gan they make,
That erthe and see, and tree, and every lake
So ful was, that unnethe was ther space
For me to stonde, so ful was al the place.

And right as Aleyn, in the Pleynt of Kinde,
Devyseth Nature of aray and face,
In swich aray men mighten hir ther finde.
This noble emperesse, ful of grace,
Bad every foul to take his owne place,
As they were wont alwey fro yeer to yere,
Seynt Valentynes day, to stonden there.

That is to sey, the foules of ravyne
Were hyest set; and than the foules smale,
That eten as hem nature wolde enclyne,

Thorgh me men goon, than spak that
other syde,
Unto the mortal strokes of the spere,
Of which Disdayn and Daunger is the gyde,
Ther tree shal never fruyt ne leves bere.
This streem you ledeth to the sorwful were,
Ther as the fish in prison is al drye;
Theschewing is only the remedye.

Thise vers of gold and blak ywriten were,
The whiche I gan a stounde to beholde,
For with that oon encresed ay my fere,
And with that other gan myn herte bolde;
That oon me hette, that other did me colde,
No wit had I, for errour, for to chese,
To entre or flee, or me to save or lese.

Right as, betwixen adamauntes two
Of even might, a pece of iren yset,
That hath no might to meve to ne fro,
For what that on may hale, that other let,
Ferde I, that niste whether me was bet,
To entre or leve, til African my gyde
Me hente, and shoof in at the gates wyde,

And seyde: Hit stondeth writen in thy face,
Thyn errour, though thou telle it not to me;
But dred thee nat to come into this place,

For this wryting is nothing ment by thee,
Ne by noon, but he Loves servant be;
For thou of love hast lost thy tast, I gesse,
As seek man hath of swete and bitternesse.

But natheles, although that thou be dulle,
Yit that thou canst not do, yit mayst thou
see;
For many a man that may not stonde a pulle,
Yit lyketh him at the wrastling for to be,
And demeth yit wher he do bet or he;
And if thou haddest cunning for tendyte,
I shal thee shewen mater of to wryte.

With that my hond in his he took anoon,
Of which I comfort caughte, and wente in
faste;
But lord! so I was glad and wel begoon!
For overal, wher that I myn eyen caste,
Were treës clad with leves that ay shal laste,
Eche in his kinde, of colour fresh and grene
As emeraude, that joye was to sene.

The bilder ook, and eek the hardy asshe;
The piler elm, the cofre unto careyne;
The boxtree piper; holm to whippes lasshe;
The sayling firr; the cipres, deth to pleyne;
The sheter ew, the asp for shaftes pleyne;

To you speke I, ye tercelets, quod Nature,
Beth of good herte and serveth, alle three;
A yere is not so longe to endure,
And ech of yow peyne him, in his degree,
For to do wel; for, God wot, quit is she
Fro yow this yeer; what after so befalle,
This entremes is dressed for you alle.

And whan this werk al broght was to an
ende,
To every foule Nature yaf his make
By even acorde, and on hir wey they wende.
A! lord! the blisse and joye that they make!
For ech of hem gan other in winges take,
And with hir nekkes ech gan other winde,
Thanking alwey the noble goddesse of
kinde.

But first were chosen foules for to singe,
As yeer by yere was alwey hir usaunce
To singe a roundel at hir departinge,
To do Nature honour and plesaunce.
The note, I trowe, maked was in Fraunce;
The wordes wer swich as ye may heer finde,
The nexte vers, as I now have in minde.

Qui bien aime a tard oublie.
Now welcom somer, with thy sonne softe,

That hast this wintres weders over-shake,
And driven awey the longe nightes blake!

Seynt Valentyn, that art ful hy on-lofte;
Thus singen smale foules for thy sake,
Now welcom somer, with thy sonne
softe,
That hast this wintres weders over-shake.

Wel han they cause for to gladen ofte,
Sith ech of hem recovered hath his make;
Ful blisful may they singen whan they
wake;
Now welcom somer, with thy sonne softe,
That hast this wintres weders over-shake,
And driven awey the longe nightes blake.

And with the showting, whan hir song
was do,
That foules maden at hir flight away,
I wook, and other bokes took me to
To rede upon, and yet I rede alway;
I hope, ywis, to rede so som day
That I shal mete som thing for to fare
The bet; and thus to rede I nil not spare.

Explicit tractatus de congregacione Volu-
crum die sancti Valentini.

BOETHIUS DE CONSOLATIONE PHILOSOPHIE ✤ BOOK I. ✤

Metre I. ✤✤✤✤✤✤✤✤✤✤✤✤✤✤
Carmina qui quondam studio florente peregi.

I, WEPING, AM CONSTREINED TO biginnen vers of sorowful matere, that whylom in florisching studie made delitable ditees. for lo! rendinge Muses of poetes endyten to me thinges to be writen; and drery vers of wrecchednesse weten my face with verray teres. At the leeste, no drede ne mighte overcomen tho Muses, that they ne weren felawes, and folweden my wey, that is to seyn, whan I was exyled; they that weren glorie of my youthe, whylom weleful and grene, comforten now the sorowful werdes of me, olde man ✐ for elde is comen unwarly upon me, hasted by the harmes that I have, and sorow hath comaunded his age to be in me. Heres hore ben shad overtymeliche upon myn heved, & the slake skin trembleth upon myn empted body. Thilke deeth of men is weleful that ne cometh not in yeres that ben swete, but cometh to wrecches, often ycleped.

ALLAS! allas! with how deef an ere deeth, cruel, torneth awey fro wrecches, and naiteth to closen wepinge eyen! Whyl fortune, unfeithful, favorede me with lighte goodes, the sorowful houre, that is to seyn, the deeth, hadde almost dreynt myn heved. But now, for fortune cloudy hath chaunged hir deceyvable chere to meward, myn unpitous lyf draweth along unagreable

Ne may of hit non other weyes witen,
But as he hath herd seyd, or founde hit writen;
for by assay ther may no man hit preve.
But goddes forbode, but men shulde leve
Wel more thing then men han seen with yë!
Men shal nat wenen everything a lyë
for that he seigh it nat of yore ago.
God wot, a thing is never the lesse so
Thogh every wight ne may hit nat ysee.
Bernard the monk ne saugh nat al, parde!

THAN mote we to bokes that we finde,
Through which that olde thinges been in minde,
And to the doctrine of these olde wyse,
Yeven credence, in every skilful wyse,
And trowen on these olde aproved stories
Of holinesse, of regnes, of victories,
Of love, of hate, of other sundry thinges,
Of whiche I may not maken rehersinges.
And if that olde bokes were aweye,
Yloren were of remembraunce the keye.
Wel oghte us than on olde bokes leve,
Theras ther is non other assay by preve.

AND, as for me, though that my wit be lyte,
On bokes for to rede I me delyte,

A THOUSAND SYTHES HAVE I HERD
men telle,
That ther is joye in heven, and peyne in helle;
And I acorde wel that hit be so;
But natheles, this wot I wel also,
That ther nis noon that dwelleth in this contree,
That either hath in helle or heven ybe,

the souning windes moeven and bisien the
smothe water of the see; & what spirit torneth the stable hevene; and why the sterre
aryseth out of the rede eest, to fallen in the
westrene wawes; and what atempreth the
lusty houres of the firste somer sesoun,
that highteth and apparaileth the erthe with
rosene flowres; and who maketh that plen-
tevouse autompne, in fulle yeres, fleteth with
hevy grapes. And eek this man was wont to
telle the dyverse causes of nature that weren
yhidde. Allas! now lyeth he empted of light
of his thought; & his nekke is pressed with
hevy cheynes; and bereth his chere enclyned
adoun for the grete weighte, & is constreined to looken on the fool erthe!

Prose II.

Set medicine, inquit, tempus est.

AT tyme is now, quod
she, of medicine more
than of compleinte,
forsothe than she en-
tendinge to meward
with alle the lookinge
of hir eyen, seide: Art
nat thou he, quod she,
that whylom ynoris-
shed with my milk, &

fostered with myne metes, were escaped and
comen to corage of a parfit man? Certes, I yaf
thee swiche armures that, yif thou thyself ne
haddest first cast hem awey, they shulden han
defended thee in sikernesse that may nat ben
overcomen. Knowest thou me nat? Why art
thou stille? Is it for shame or for astoninge?
It were me lever that it were for shame; but
it semeth me that astoninge hath oppressed thee And whan she say me nat only
stille, but withouten office of tunge & al doumb,
she leide hir hand softely upon my brest, and
seide: Here nis no peril, quod she; he is fallen
into a litargie, whiche that is a comune syke-
nes to hertes that ben deceived. He hath a litel
foryeten himself, but certes he shal lightly
remembren himself, yif so be that he hath
knowen me or now; & that he may so don, I
wil wypen a litel his eyen, that ben derked by
the cloude of mortal thinges Thise wordes
seide she, and with the lappe of hir garment,
yplyted in a frounce, she dryede myn eyen,
that weren fulle of the wawes of my wepinges.

Metre III.

Tunc me discussa liquerunt nocte tenebre.

THUS, whan that night was discussed
& chased awey, derknesses forleften
me, and to myn eyen repeirede ayein

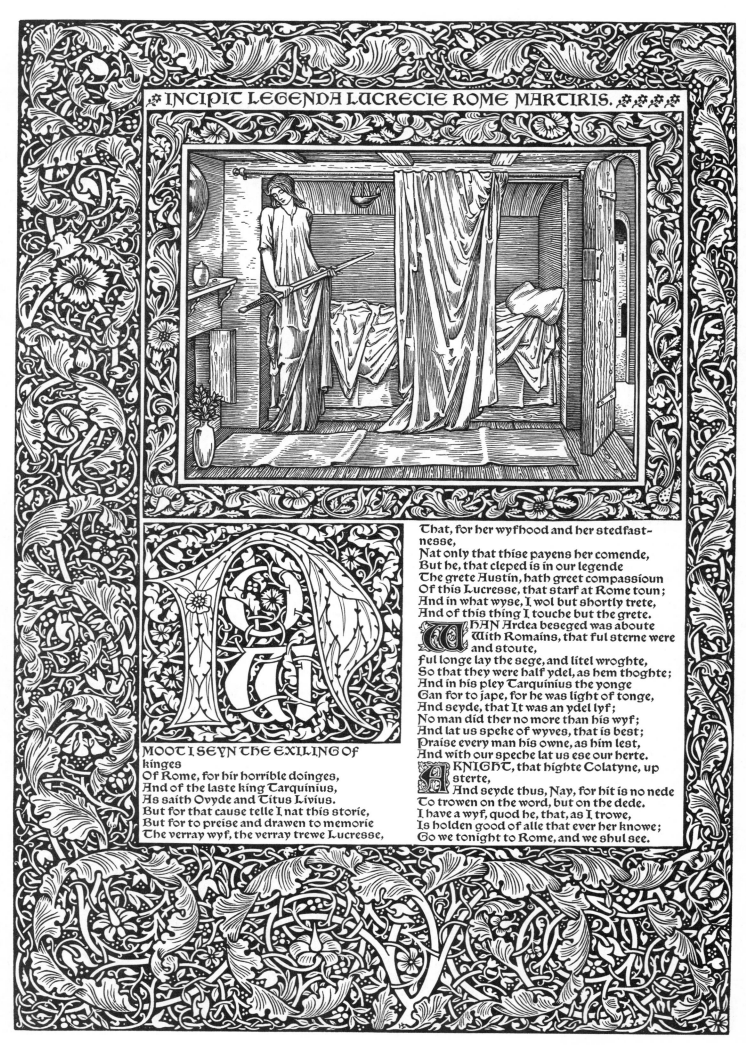

INCIPIT LEGENDA LUCRECIE ROME MARTIRIS. ✤✤✤✤

NOOT I SEYN THE EXILING OF
kinges
Of Rome, for hir horrible doinges,
And of the laste king Tarquinius,
As saith Ovyde and Titus Livius.
But for that cause telle I nat this storie,
But for to preise and drawen to memorie
The verray wyf, the verray trewe Lucresse,

That, for her wyfhood and her stedfast-
nesse,
Nat only that thise payens her comende,
But he, that cleped is in our legende
The grete Austin, hath greet compassioun
Of this Lucresse, that starf at Rome toun;
And in what wyse, I wol but shortly trete,
And of this thing I touche but the grete.

WHAN Ardea beseged was aboute
With Romains, that ful sterne were
and stoute,
Ful longe lay the sege, and litel wroghte,
So that they were half ydel, as hem thoghte;
And in his pley Tarquinius the yonge
Gan for to jape, for he was light of tonge,
And seyde, that It was an ydel lyf;
No man did ther no more than his wyf;
And lat us speke of wyves, that is best;
Praise every man his owne, as him lest,
And with our speche lat us ese our herte.

A KNIGHT, that highte Colatyne, up
sterte,
And seyde thus, Nay, for hit is no nede
To trowen on the word, but on the dede.
I have a wyf, quod he, that, as I trowe,
Is holden good of alle that ever her knowe;
Go we tonight to Rome, and we shul see.

I HAVE GRET WONDER, BY THIS LIGHTE,
How that I live, for day ne nighte
I may nat slepe wel nigh noght;
I have so many an ydel thoght
Purely for defaute of slepe,
That, by my trouthe, I take kepe
Of nothing, how hit cometh or goth,
Ne me nis nothing leef nor loth.

Al is yliche good to me,
Joye or sorowe, wherso hit be,
For I have feling in nothing,
But, as it were, a mased thing,
Alway in point to falle adoun;
For sory imaginacioun
Is alway hoolly in my minde.
AND wel ye wite, agaynes kinde
Hit were to liven in this wyse;
For nature wolde nat suffyse
To noon erthely creature
Not longe tyme to endure
Withoute slepe, and been in sorwe;
And I ne may, ne night ne morwe,
Slepe; and thus melancolye,
And dreed I have for to dye,
Defaute of slepe, and hevinesse
Hath sleyn my spirit of quiknesse,
That I have lost al lustihede.
Suche fantasyes ben in myn hede
So I not what is best to do.
BUT men mighte axe me, why so
I may not slepe, and what me is?
But natheles, who aske this
Leseth his asking trewely.
Myselven can not telle why
The sooth; but trewely, as I gesse,

But atte laste of Tarquiny she hem tolde,
This rewful cas, and al this thing horrible.
The wo to tellen hit were impossible,
That she and alle her frendes made atones.
Al hadde folkes hertes been of stones,
Hit mighte have maked hem upon her rewe,
Her herte was so wyfly and so trewe.
She seide, that, for her gilt ne for her blame,
Her husbond sholde nat have the foule name,
That wolde she nat suffre, by no wey.
And they answerden alle, upon hir fey,
That they foryeve hit her, for hit was right;
Hit was no gilt, hit lay nat in her might;
And seiden her ensamples many oon.
But al for noght; for thus she seide anoon:
Be as be may, quod she, of forgiving,
I wol nat have no forgift for nothing.
But prively she caughte forth a knyf,
And therwithal she rafte herself her lyf;
And as she fel adoun, she caste her look,
And of her clothes yit she hede took;
for in her falling yit she hadde care
Lest that her feet or swiche thing lay bare;
So wel she loved clennesse and eek trouthe.
Of her had al the toun of Rome routhe,

And Brutus by her chaste blode hath swore
That Tarquin sholde ybanisht be therfore,
And al his kin; and let the peple calle,
And openly the tale he tolde hem alle,
And openly let carie her on a bere
Through al the toun, that men may see & here
The horrible deed of her oppressioun.
Ne never was ther king in Rome toun
Sin thilke day; and she was holden there
A seint, and ever her day yhalwed dere
As in hir lawe: and thus endeth Lucresse,
The noble wyf, as Titus bereth witnesse.
I TELL hit, for she was of love so trewe,
Ne in her wille she chaunged for no newe.
And for the stable herte, sad and kinde,
That in these women men may alday finde;
Ther as they caste hir herte, ther hit dwelleth.
for wel I wot, that Crist himselve telleth,
That in Israel, as wyd as is the lond,
That so gret feith in al the lond he ne fond
As in a woman; and this is no lye.
And as of men, loketh which tirannye
They doon alday; assay hem who so liste,
The trewest is ful brotel for to triste.

Explicit Legenda Lucrecie Rome martiris.

INCIPIT LEGENDA ADRIANE DE ATHENES

IUGE INFERNAL, MINOS,
OF CRETE KING,
NOW COMETH THY LOT,
NOW COMESTOW ON THE
RING;
NAT FOR THY SAKE ONLY
WRYTE I THIS STORIE,
BUT FOR TO CLEPE A-
GEIN UNTO MEMORIE
OF THESEUS THE GRETE
UNTROUTHE OF LOVE;
FOR WHICH THE GODDES
OF THE HEVEN ABOVE
BEN WROTHE, AND
WRECHE HAN TAKE FOR
THY SINNE.
BE REED FOR SHAME!
NOW I THY LYF BE-
GINNE.

MINOS, that was the mighty king of
Crete,
That hadde an hundred citees
stronge and grete,
To scole hath sent his sone Androgeus,
To Athenes; of the whiche hit happed thus,
That he was slayn, lerning philosophye,
Right in that citee, nat but for envye.

THE grete Minos, of the whiche I speke,
His sones deeth is comen for to wreke;
Alcathoe he bisegeth harde and longe.
But natheles the walles be so stronge,
And Nisus, that was king of that citee,
So chivalrous, that litel dredeth he;
Of Minos or his ost took he no cure,

Til on a day befel an aventure,
That Nisus doghter stood upon the wal,
And of the sege saw the maner al.
So happed hit, that, at a scarmishing,
She caste her herte upon Minos the king,
for his beautee and for his chivalrye,
So sore, that she wende for to dye.
And, shortly of this proces for to pace,
She made Minos winnen thilke place,
So that the citee was al at his wille,
To saven whom him list, or elles spille;
But wikkedly he quitte her kindenesse,
And let her drenche in sorowe and distresse
Nere that the goddes hadde of her pite;
But that tale were to long as now for me.

ATHENES wan this king Minos also,
And Alcathoe and other tounes mo;
And this theffect, that Minos hath so
driven
Hem of Athenes, that they mote him yiven
fro yere to yere her owne children dere
for to be slayn, as ye shul after here.

THIS Minos hath a monstre, a wikked
beste,
That was so cruel that, without areste,
Whan that a man was broght in his presence,
He wolde him ete, ther helpeth no defence.
And every thridde yeer, withouten doute,
They casten lot, and, as hit com aboute
On riche, on pore, he moste his sone take,
And of his child he moste present make
Unto Minos, to save him or to spille,
Or lete his beste devoure him at his wille.
And this hath Minos don, right in despyt;
To wreke his sone was set al his delyt,

LITTLE LOWIS MY SONE, I HAVE PERCEIVED wel by certeyne evidences thyn abilite to lerne sciencez touchinge noumbres and proporciouns; & as wel considere I thy bisy preyere in special to lerne the Tretis of the Astrolabie. Than, for as mechel as a philosofre seith, He wrappeth him in his frend, that condescendeth to the rightful preyers of his frend, ther-

for have I geven thee a suffisaunt Astrolabie as for oure orizonte, compowned after the latitude of Oxenford; upon which, by mediacion of this litel tretis, I purpose to teche thee a certein nombre of conclusions apertening to the same instrument. I seye a certein of conclusiouns, for three causes. The furste cause is this: truste wel that alle the conclusiouns that han ben founde, or elles possibly mighten be founde in so noble an instrument as an Astrolabie, ben unknowe perfitly to any mortal man in this regioun, as I suppose. Another cause is this; that sothly, in any tretis of the Astrolabie that I have seyn, there ben some conclusions that wole nat in alle thinges performen hir bihestes; & some of hem ben to harde to thy tendre age of ten yeer to conseyve. This tretis, divided in fyve parties, wole I shewe thee under ful lighte rewles & naked wordes in English; for Latin ne canstow yit but smal, my lyte sone. But natheles, suffise to thee thise trewe conclusiouns in English, as wel as suffyseth to thise noble clerkes Grekes thise same conclusiouns in Greek, & to Arabiens in Arabik, and to Jewes in Ebrew, & to the Latin folk in Latin; whiche Latin folk han hem furst out of othre diverse

for on a night, slepinge, he let her lye,
And stal awey unto his companye,
And, as a traitour, forth he gan to saile
Toward the large contree of Itaile.
Thus hath he laft Dido in wo and pyne;
And wedded ther a lady hight Lavyne.

A CLOTH he lafte, and eek his swerd
stonding,
Whan he fro Dido stal in her sleping,
Right at her beddes heed, so gan he hye
Whan that he stal awey to his navye;
Which cloth, whan sely Dido gan awake,
She hath hit kist ful ofte for his sake;
And seide: O cloth, whyl Jupiter hit leste,
Tak now my soule, unbind me of this unreste!
I have fulfild of fortune al the cours.
And thus, allas! withouten his socours,
Twenty tyme yswowned hath she thanne.
And, whan that she unto her suster Anne
Compleyned had, of which I may nat wryte,
So greet a routhe I have hit for tendyte,
And bad her norice and her suster goon
To fecchen fyr and other thing anoon,
And seide, that she wolde sacrifye.

And, whan she mighte her tyme wel espye,
Upon the fyr of sacrifys she sterte,
And with his swerd she roof her to the herte.

BUT, as myn autour seith, right thus
she seyde;
Or she was hurt, before that she deyde,
She wroot a lettre anoon, that thus began:
Right so, quod she, as that the whyte
swan
Ayeins his deeth beginneth for to singe,
Right so to yow make I my compleyninge.
Nat that I trowe to geten yow again,
For wel I woot that it is al in vain,
Sin that the goddes been contraire to me.
But sin my name is lost through yow, quod
she,
I may wel lese a word on yow, or letter,
Albeit that I shal be never the better;
For thilke wind that blew your ship awey,
The same wind hath blowe awey your fey.
But who wol al this letter have in minde,
Rede Ovide, and in him he shal hit finde.
Explicit Legenda Didonis martiris, Carta-
ginis regine.

INCIPIT LEGENDA YSIPHILE ET MEDEE MARTIRUM.

Have at thee, Jasoun! now thyn horn is blowe!
But certes, hit is bothe routhe and wo
That love with false loveres werketh so;
For they shul have wel better love and chere
Than he that hath aboght his love ful dere,
Or had in armes many a blody box.
For ever as tendre a capoun et the fox,
Thogh he be fals and hath the foul betrayed,
As shal the goodman that therfor hath payed;
Al have he to the capoun skille and right,
The false fox wol have his part at night.
On Jasoun this ensample is wel ysene
By Isiphile and Medea the quene.

IN Tessalye, as Guido telleth us,
Ther was a king that highte Pelleus,
That had a brother, which that highte
Eson;
And, whan for age he mighte unnethes gon,
He yaf to Pelleus the governing
Of al his regne, and made him lord and king.
Of which Eson this Jasoun geten was,
That, in his tyme, in al that lond, ther nas
Nat swich a famous knight of gentilesse,
Of freedom, & of strengthe and lustinesse.
After his fader deeth, he bar him so
That ther nas noon that liste been his fo,
But dide him al honour and companye;
Of which this Pelleus hath greet envye,
Imagining that Jasoun mighte be
Enhaunsed so, and put in swich degree
With love of lordes of his regioun,
That from his regne he may be put adoun.
And in his wit, anight, compassed he
How Jasoun mighte best destroyed be
Withoute slaunder of his compasment.

ROTE OF FALSE LOVERS, DUK JA-
SOUN!
Thou sly devourer and confusioun
Of gentilwommen, tender creatures,
Thou madest thy reclaiming and thy lures
To ladies of thy statly apparaunce,
And of thy wordes, farced with plesaunce,
And of thy feyned trouthe and thy manere,
With thyn obeisaunce and thy humble chere,
And with thy counterfeted peyne and wo.
Ther other falsen oon, thou falsest two!
Of ofte swore thou that thou woldest dye
For love, whan thou ne feltest maladye
Save foul delyt, which that thou callest love!
If that I live, thy name shal be shove
In English, that thy sleighte shal be knowe!

Hir whyte coroun berth of hit witnesse;
for also many vertues hadde she,
As smale floures in hir coroun be.
In remembraunce of hir and in honour,
Cibella made the dayesy and the flour
Ycoroned al with whyt, as men may see;
And Mars yaf to hir coroun reed, pardee,
In stede of rubies, set among the whyte.

HERWITH this quene wex reed for shame a lyte,
Whan she was preysed so in hir presence.
Than seyde Love: A ful gret negligence
Was hit to thee, to write unstedfastnesse
Of women, sith thou knowest hir goodnesse
By preef, and eek by stories heerbiforn;
Let be the chaf, and wryt wel of the corn.
Why noldest thou han writen of Alceste,

And leten Criseide been aslepe and reste?
for of Alceste shulde thy wryting be,
Sin that thou wost that kalender is she
Of goodnesse, for she taughte of fyn lovinge,
And namely of wyfhood the livinge,
And alle the boundes that she oghte kepe;
Thy litel wit was thilke tyme aslepe.
But now I charge thee, upon thy lyf,
That in thy Legend thou make of this wyf,
Whan thou hast othere smale mad before;
And fare now wel, I charge thee no more.
At Cleopatre I wol that thou beginne;
And so forth; and my love so shalt thou winne.

And with that word of sleep I gan awake,
And right thus on my Legend gan I make.
Explicit prohemium.

⁕⁕ INCIPIT LEGENDA CLEOPATRIE MARTIRIS, EGIPTI REGINE ⁕⁕⁕⁕⁕⁕⁕⁕⁕⁕⁕⁕⁕⁕⁕⁕⁕⁕⁕⁕⁕⁕⁕⁕⁕

THE DEETH OF THOLOMEE THE king,
That al Egipte hadde in his governing,
Regned his quene Cleopataras;
Til on a tyme befel ther swiche a cas,
That out of Rome was sent a senatour,
for to conqueren regnes and honour
Unto the toun of Rome, as was usaunce,
To have the world unto her obeisaunce,
And, sooth to seye, Antonius was his name.
So fil hit, as fortune him oghte a shame
Whan he was fallen in prosperitee,
Rebel unto the toun of Rome is he.
And over al this, the suster of Cesar,
He lafte hir falsly, er that she was war,
And wolde algates han another wyf;
for whiche he took with Rome and Cesar stryf.

NATHELES, forsooth, this ilke senatour
Was a ful worthy gentil werreyour,

And of his deeth hit was ful greet damage.
But love had broght this man in swiche a rage,
And him so narwe bounden in his las,
Al for the love of Cleopataras,
That al the world he sette at no value.
Him thoughte, nas to him no thing so due
As Cleopatras for to love and serve;
Him roghte nat in armes for to sterve
In the defence of hir, and of hir right.

THIS noble quene eek lovede so this knight,
Through his desert, & for his chivalrye;
As certeinly, but if that bokes lye,
He was, of persone and of gentilesse,
And of discrecioun and hardinesse,
Worthy to any wight that liven may.
And she was fair as is the rose in May.
And, for to maken shortly is the beste,
She wex his wyf, and hadde him as hir leste.

THE wedding and the feste to devyse,
To me, that have ytake swiche empryse
Of so many a storie for to make,
Hit were to long, lest that I sholde slake
Of thing that bereth more effect and charge;
for men may overlade a ship or barge;
And forthy to theffect than wol I skippe,
And al the remenant, I wol lete hit slippe.

OCTOVIAN, that wood was of this dede,
Shoop him an ost on Antony to lede
Al outerly for his destruccioun,
With stoute Romains, cruel as leoun;
To ship they wente, and thus I let hem saile.

ANTONIUS was war, and wol nat faile
To meten with thise Romains, if he may;
Took eek his reed, and bothe, upon a day,
His wyf and he, and al his ost, forth wente

To shippe anoon, no lenger they ne stente;
And in the see hit happed hem to mete,
Up goth the trompe, and for to shoute and shete,
And peynen hem to sette on with the sonne.
With grisly soun out goth the grete gonne,
And heterly they hurtlen al at ones,
And fro the top doun cometh the grete stones.
In goth the grapenel so ful of crokes
Among the ropes, and the shering-hokes.
In with the polax presseth he and he;
Behind the mast beginneth he to flee,
And out agayn, and dryveth him overborde;
He stingeth him upon his speres orde;
He rent the sail with hokes lyke a sythe;
He bringeth the cuppe, and biddeth hem be blythe;
He poureth pesen upon the hacches slider;
With pottes ful of lym they goon togider;
And thus the longe day in fight they spende
Til, at the laste, as every thing hath ende,
Antony is shent, and put him to the flighte,
And al his folk togo, that best go mighte.

FLEETH eek the queen, with al hir purpre sail,
for strokes, which that wente as thikke as hail;
No wonder was, she mighte hit nat endure.
And whan that Antony saw that aventure,
Allas! quod he, the day that I was born!
My worshipe in this day thus have I lorn!
And for dispeyr out of his witte he sterte,
And roof himself anoon throughout the herte
Er that he ferther wente out of the place.
His wyf, that coude of Cesar have no grace,
To Egipte is fled, for drede & for distresse;
But herkneth, ye that speke of kindenesse.

YE men, that falsly sweren many an ooth
That ye wol dye, if that your love be wrooth,
Heer may ye seen of women whiche a trouthe!
This woful Cleopatre hath mad swich routhe
That ther nis tonge noon that may hit telle.
But on the morwe she wol no lenger dwelle,
But made hir subtil werkmen make a shryne
Of alle the rubies and the stones fyne
In al Egipte that she coude espye;
And putte ful the shryne of spycerye,
And leet the cors embaume; & forth she fette
This dede cors, and in the shryne hit shette.
And next the shryne a pit than doth she grave;
And alle the serpents that she mighte have,

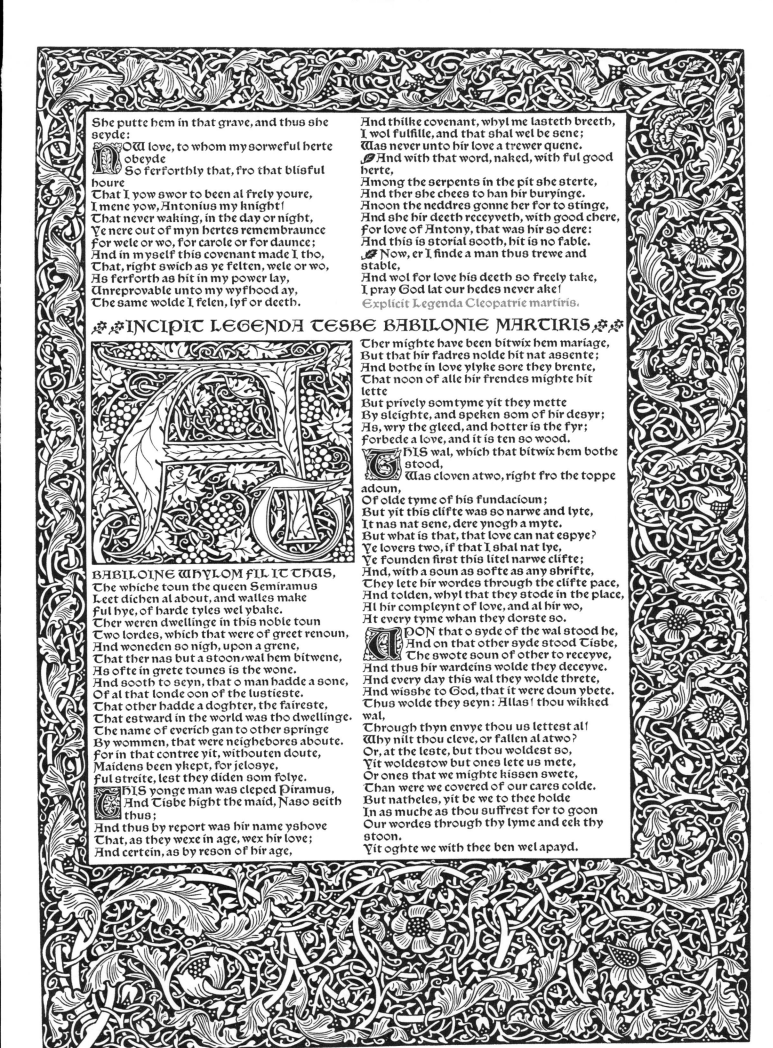

She putte hem in that grave, and thus she seyde:
NOW love, to whom my sorweful herte obeyde
So ferforthly that, fro that blisful houre
That I yow swor to been al frely youre,
I mene yow, Antonius my knight!
That never waking, in the day or night,
Ye nere out of myn hertes remembraunce
For wele or wo, for carole or for daunce;
And in myself this covenant made I tho,
That, right swich as ye felten, wele or wo,
As ferforth as hit in my power lay,
Unreprovable unto my wyfhood ay,
The same wolde I felen, lyf or deeth.

And thilke covenant, whyl me lasteth breeth,
I wol fulfille, and that shal wel be sene;
Was never unto hir love a trewer quene.
And with that word, naked, with ful good herte,
Among the serpents in the pit she sterte,
And ther she chees to han hir buryinge.
Anoon the neddres gonne her for to stinge,
And she hir deeth receyveth, with good chere,
For love of Antony, that was hir so dere:
And this is storial sooth, hit is no fable.
Now, er I finde a man thus trewe and stable,
And wol for love his deeth so freely take,
I pray God lat our hedes never ake!
Explicit Legenda Cleopatrie martiris.

❧ INCIPIT LEGENDA TESBE BABILONIE MARTIRIS ❧

BABILOINE WHYLOM FIL IT THUS,
The whiche toun the queen Semiramus
Leet dichen al about, and walles make
Ful hye, of harde tyles wel ybake.
Ther weren dwellinge in this noble toun
Two lordes, which that were of greet renoun,
And woneden so nigh, upon a grene,
That ther nas but a stoon-wal hem bitwene,
As ofte in grete tounes is the wone.
And sooth to seyn, that o man hadde a sone,
Of al that londe oon of the lustieste.
That other hadde a doghter, the faireste,
That estward in the world was tho dwellinge.
The name of everich gan to other springe
By wommen, that were neighebores aboute.
For in that contree yit, withouten doute,
Maidens been ykept, for jelosye,
Ful streite, lest they diden som folye.
THIS yonge man was cleped Piramus,
And Tisbe hight the maid, Naso seith thus;
And thus by report was hir name yshove
That, as they wexe in age, wex hir love;
And certein, as by reson of hir age,

Ther mighte have been bitwix hem mariage,
But that hir fadres nolde hit nat assente;
And bothe in love ylyke sore they brente,
That noon of alle hir frendes mighte hit lette
But prively somtyme yit they mette
By sleighte, and speken som of hir desyr;
As, wry the gleed, and hotter is the fyr;
Forbede a love, and it is ten so wood.
THIS wal, which that bitwix hem bothe stood,
Was cloven atwo, right fro the toppe adoun,
Of olde tyme of his fundacioun;
But yit this clifte was so narwe and lyte,
It nas nat sene, dere ynogh a myte.
But what is that, that love can nat espye?
Ye lovers two, if that I shal nat lye,
Ye founden first this litel narwe clifte;
And, with a soun as softe as any shrifte,
They lete hir wordes through the clifte pace,
And tolden, whyl that they stode in the place,
Al hir compleynt of love, and al hir wo,
At every tyme whan they dorste so.
UPON that o syde of the wal stood he,
And on that other syde stood Tisbe,
The swote soun of other to receyve,
And thus hir wardeins wolde they deceyve.
And every day this wal they wolde threte,
And wisshe to God, that it were doun ybete.
Thus wolde they seyn: Allas! thou wikked wal,
Through thyn envye thou us lettest al!
Why nilt thou cleve, or fallen al atwo?
Or, at the leste, but thou woldest so,
Yit woldestow but ones lete us mete,
Or ones that we mighte kissen swete,
Than were we covered of our cares colde.
But natheles, yit be we to thee holde
In as muche as thou suffrest for to goon
Our wordes through thy lyme and eek thy stoon.
Yit oghte we with thee ben wel apayd.

AND whan thise ydel wordes weren sayd,
The colde wal they wolden kisse of stoon,
And take hir leve, & forth they wolden goon.
And this was gladly in the eventyde
Or wonder erly, lest men hit espyde;
And longe tyme they wroghte in this manere
Til on a day, whan Phebus gan to clere,
Aurora with the stremes of hir hete
Had dryed up the dew of herbes wete;
Unto this clifte, as it was wont to be,
Com Pyramus, and after com Tisbe,
And plighten trouthe fully in hir fey
That ilke same night to stele awey,
And to begyle hir wardeins everichoon,
And forth out of the citee for to goon;
And, for the feldes been so brode and wyde,
For to mete in o place at o tyde,
They sette mark hir meting sholde be
Ther king Ninus was graven, under a tree;
For olde payens that ydoles heried
Useden tho in feldes to ben beried;
And faste by this grave was a welle.
And, shortly of this tale for to telle,
This covenant was affermed wonder faste;
And longe hem thoughte that the sonne laste,
That hit nere goon under the see adoun.

THIS Tisbe hath so greet affeccioun
And so greet lyking Piramus to see,
That, whan she seigh her tyme mighte be,
At night she stal awey ful prively
With her face ywimpled subtilly;
For alle her frendes, for to save her trouthe,
She hath forsake; allas! and that is routhe
That ever woman wolde be so trewe
To trusten man, but she the bet him knewe!
And to the tree she goth a ful good pas,
For love made her so hardy in this cas;
And by the welle adoun she gan her dresse.
Allas! than comth a wilde leonesse
Out of the wode, withouten more areste,
With blody mouthe, of strangling of a beste,
To drinken of the welle, ther as she sat;
And, whan that Tisbe had espyed that,
She rist hir up, with a ful drery herte,
And in a cave with dredful foot she sterte,
For by the mone she seigh hit wel withalle.
And, as she ran, her wimpel leet she falle,
And took noon heed, so sore she was awhaped,
And eek so glad of that she was escaped;

And at the laste he took avisement
To senden him into some fer contree
Ther as this Jasoun may destroyed be.
This was his wit; al made he to Jasoun
Gret chere of love and of affeccioun,
For drede lest his lordes hit espyde.
So fil hit so, as fame renneth wyde,
Ther was swich tyding overal and swich los,
That in an yle that called was Colcos,
Beyonde Troye, estward in the see,
That therin was a ram, that men mighte see,
That had a flees of gold, that shoon so
brighte,
That nowher was ther swich another sighte;
But hit was kept alway with a dragoun,
And many othere merveils, up and doun,
And with two boles, maked al of bras,
That spitten fyr, and moche thing ther was.
But this was eek the tale, nathelees,
That whoso wolde winne thilke flees,
He moste bothe, or he hit winne mighte,
With the boles and the dragoun fighte;
And king Oëtes lord was of that yle.
THIS Pelleus bethoghte upon this
wyle;
That he his nevew Jasoun wolde
enhorte
To sailen to that lond, him to disporte,

And seide: Nevew, if hit mighte be
That swich a worship mighte fallen thee,
That thou this famous tresor mightest
winne,
And bringen hit my regioun withinne,
Hit were to me gret plesaunce and honour;
Than were I holde to quyte thy labour.
And al the cost I wol myselven make;
And chees what folk that thou wilt with thee
take;
Lat see now, darstow taken this viage?
Jasoun was yong, and lusty of corage,
And undertook to doon this ilke empryse.
ANOON Argus his shippes gan devyse;
With Jasoun wente the stronge
Ercules,
And many another that he with him chees.
But whoso axeth who is with him gon,
Lat him go reden Argonauticon,
For he wol telle a tale long ynow.
Philotetes anoon the sail updrow,
Whan that the wind was good, and gan him
hye
Out of his contree called Tessalye.
So long he sailed in the salte see
Til in the yle Lemnoun aryved he,
Al be this nat rehersed of Guido,
Yet seith Ovyde in his Epistles so.

INCIPIT LEGENDA DIDONIS MARTIRIS, CARTAGINIS REGINE

AND HONOUR, VIRGIL MANTUAN,
Be to thy name! and I shal, as I can,
folow thy lantern, as thou gost biforn,
How Eneas to Dido was forsworn.
In thyn Eneid and Naso wol I take
The tenour, and the grete effectes make.

WHAN Troye broght was to de-
struccioun
By Grekes sleighte, and namely
by Sinoun,
feyning the hors y-offred to Minerve,
Through which that many a Troyan moste
sterve;
And Ector had, after his deeth, appered,
And fyr so wood, it mighte nat be stered,
In al the noble tour of Ilioun,
That of the citee was the cheef dungeoun;
And al the contree was so lowe ybroght,
And Priamus the king fordoon and noght;
And Eneas was charged by Venus
To fleen awey, he took Ascanius,
That was his sone, in his right hand, and
fledde;
And on his bakke he bar and with him ledde
His olde fader, cleped Anchises,
And by the weye his wyf Creusa he lees.
And mochel sorwe hadde he in his minde
Er that he coude his felawshippe finde.
But, at the laste, whan he had hem founde,
He made him redy in a certein stounde,
And to the see ful faste he gan him hye,

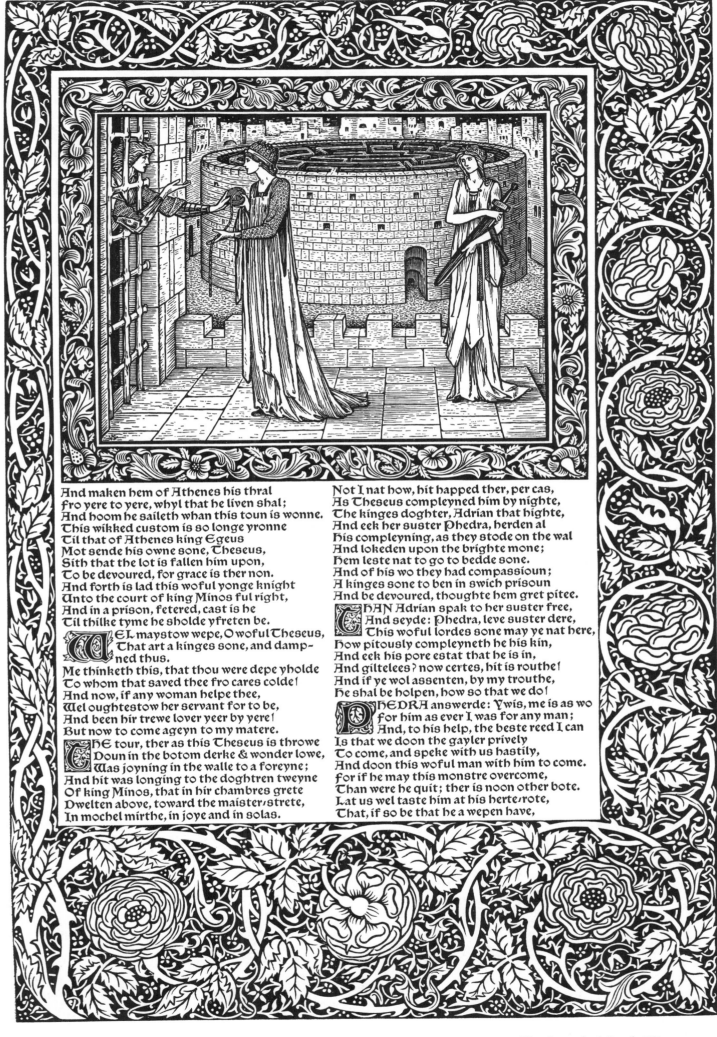

And maken hem of Athenes his thral
Fro yere to yere, whyl that he liven shal;
And hoom he saileth whan this toun is wonne.
This wikked custom is so longe yronne
Til that of Athenes king Egeus
Mot sende his owne sone, Theseus,
Sith that the lot is fallen him upon,
To be devoured, for grace is ther non.
And forth is lad this woful yonge knight
Unto the court of king Minos ful right,
And in a prison, fetered, cast is he
Til thilke tyme he sholde yfreten be.

WEL maystow wepe, O woful Theseus,
That art a kinges sone, and damp-
ned thus.
Me thinketh this, that thou were depe yholde
To whom that saved thee fro cares colde!
And now, if any woman helpe thee,
Wel oughtestow her servant for to be,
And been hir trewe lover yeer by yere!
But now to come ageyn to my matere.

THE tour, ther as this Theseus is throwe
Doun in the botom derke & wonder lowe,
Was joyning in the walle to a foreyne;
And hit was longing to the doghtren tweyne
Of king Minos, that in hir chambres grete
Dwelten above, toward the maister-strete,
In mochel mirthe, in joye and in solas.

Not I nat how, hit happed ther, per cas,
As Theseus compleyned him by nighte,
The kinges doghter, Adrian that highte,
And eek her suster Phedra, herden al
His compleyning, as they stode on the wal
And lokeden upon the brighte mone;
Hem leste nat to go to bedde sone.
And of his wo they had compassioun;
A kinges sone to ben in swich prisoun
And be devoured, thoughte hem gret pitee.

THAN Adrian spak to her suster free,
And seyde: Phedra, leve suster dere,
This woful lordes sone may ye nat here,
How pitously compleyneth he his kin,
And eek his pore estat that he is in,
And giltelees? now certes, hit is routhe!
And if ye wol assenten, by my trouthe,
He shal be holpen, how so that we do!

PHEDRA answerde: Ywis, me is as wo
For him as ever I was for any man;
And, to his help, the beste reed I can
Is that we doon the gayler prively
To come, and speke with us hastily,
And doon this woful man with him to come.
For if he may this monstre overcome,
Than were he quit; ther is noon other bote.
Lat us wel taste him at his herte-rote,
That, if so be that he a wepen have,

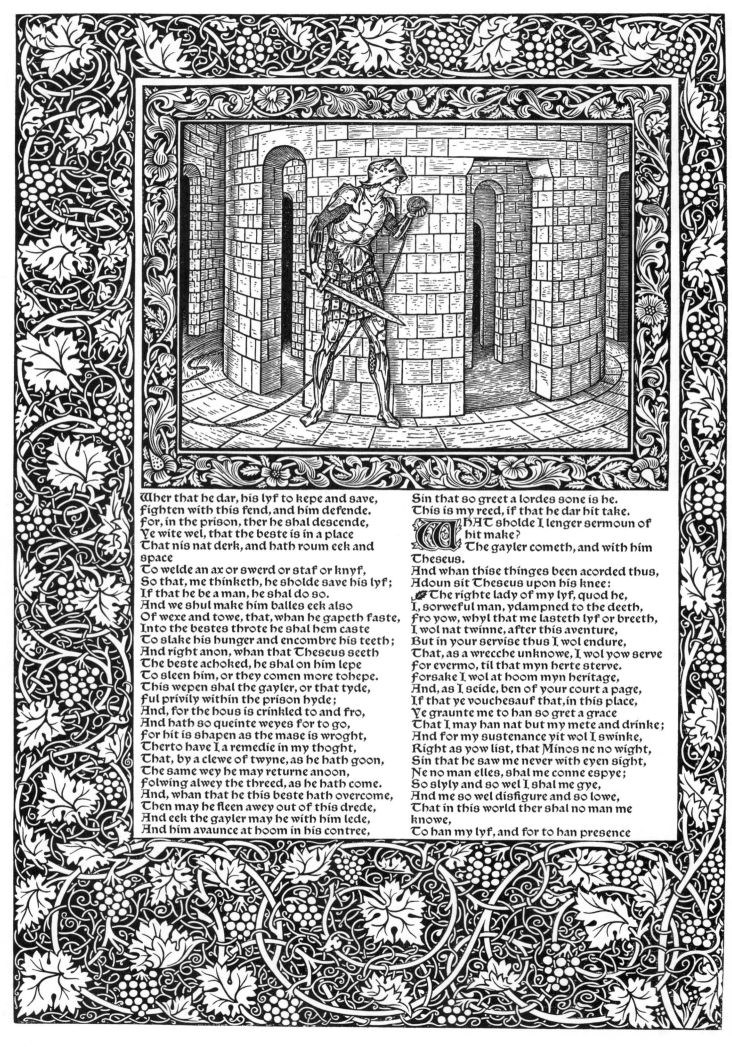

Wher that he dar, his lyf to kepe and save,
fighten with this fend, and him defende.
for, in the prison, ther he shal descende,
Ye wite wel, that the beste is in a place
That nis nat derk, and hath roum eek and
space
To welde an ax or swerd or staf or knyf,
So that, me thinketh, he sholde save his lyf;
If that he be a man, he shal do so.
And we shul make him balles eek also
Of wexe and towe, that, whan he gapeth faste,
Into the bestes throte he shal hem caste
To slake his hunger and encombre his teeth;
And right anon, whan that Theseus seeth
The beste achoked, he shal on him lepe
To sleen him, or they comen more tohepe.
This wepen shal the gayler, or that tyde,
ful privily within the prison hyde;
And, for the hous is crinkled to and fro,
And hath so queinte weyes for to go,
for hit is shapen as the mase is wroght,
Therto have I a remedie in my thoght,
That, by a clewe of twyne, as he hath goon,
The same wey he may returne anoon,
folwing alwey the threed, as he hath come.
And, whan that he this beste hath overcome,
Then may he fleen awey out of this drede,
And eek the gayler may he with him lede,
And him avaunce at hoom in his contree,

Sin that so greet a lordes sone is he.
This is my reed, if that he dar hit take.
WHAT sholde I lenger sermoun of
hit make?
The gayler cometh, and with him
Theseus.
And whan thise thinges been acorded thus,
Adoun sit Theseus upon his knee:
The righte lady of my lyf, quod he,
I, sorweful man, ydampned to the deeth,
fro yow, whyl that me lasteth lyf or breeth,
I wol nat twinne, after this aventure,
But in your servise thus I wol endure,
That, as a wrecche unknowe, I wol yow serve
for evermo, til that myn herte sterve.
forsake I wol at hoom myn heritage,
And, as I seide, ben of your court a page,
If that ye vouchesauf that, in this place,
Ye graunte me to han so greet a grace
That I may han nat but my mete and drinke;
And for my sustenance yit wol I swinke,
Right as yow list, that Minos ne no wight,
Sin that he saw me never with eyen sight,
Ne no man elles, shal me conne espye;
So slyly and so wel I shal me gye,
And me so wel disfigure and so lowe,
That in this world ther shal no man me
knowe,
To han my lyf, and for to han presence

THE remenant is no charge for to telle,
for this is al & som, thus was she served,
That never harm agilte ne deserved
Unto this cruel man, that she of wiste.
Ye may be war of men, yif that yow liste.
for, al be that he wol nat, for his shame,

Doon so as Tereus, to lese his name,
Ne serve yow as a mordrour or a knave,
ful litel whyle shul ye trewe him have,
That wol I seyn, al were he now my brother,
But hit so be that he may have non other.

INCIPIT LEGENDA PHILLIS.

That wikked fruit cometh of a wikked tree,
That may ye finde, if that it lyketh yow.
But for this ende I speke this as now,
To telle you of false Demophon.
In love a falser herde I never non,
But if hit were his fader Theseus.
God, for his grace, fro swich oon kepe us!
Thus may thise women prayen that hit here.
Now to theffect turne I of my matere.

DESTROYED is of Troye the citee;
This Demophon com sailing in the see
Toward Athenes, to his paleys large;
With him com many a ship and many a barge
ful of his folk, of which ful many oon
Is wounded sore, and seek, and wo begoon.
And they han at the sege longe ylain.
Behinde him com a wind and eek a rain
That shoof so sore, his sail ne mighte stonde,
Him were lever than al the world alonde,

PREVE AS WEL AS BY AUCTORITEE,

ME list no more to speke of him, parde;
    Thise false lovers, poison be hir bane!
    But I wol turne again to Adriane
That is with slepe for werinesse atake.
Ful sorwefully her herte may awake.
Allas! for thee my herte hath now pite!
Right in the dawening awaketh she,
And gropeth in the bedde, and fond right
    noght.
    Allas! quod she, that ever I was wroght!
I am betrayed! and her heer torente,
And to the stronde barfot faste she wente,
And cryed: Theseus! myn herte swete!
Wher be ye, that I may nat with yow mete,
And mighte thus with bestes been yslain?
    THE holwe rokkes answerde her again;
    No man she saw, and yit shyned the
    mone,
And hye upon a rokke she wente sone,
And saw his barge sailing in the see.
Cold wex her herte, and right thus seide she:
Meker than ye finde I the bestes wilde!
    Hadde he nat sinne, that her thus begylde?
She cryed: O turne again, for routhe and
    sinne!
Thy barge hath nat al his meiny inne!
    Her kerchef on a pole up stikked she,
Ascaunce that he sholde hit wel ysee,

And him remembre that she was behinde,
And turne again, and on the stronde her finde;
But al for noght; his wey he is ygoon.
And doun she fil aswown upon a stoon;
And up she rist, and kiste, in al her care,
The steppes of his feet, ther he hath fare,
And to her bedde right thus she speketh tho:
Thou bed, quod she, that hast receyved two,
Thou shalt answere of two, and nat of oon!
Wher is thy gretter part away ygoon?
Allas! wher shal I, wrecched wight, become!
For, thogh so be that ship or boot heer come,
Hoom to my contree dar I nat for drede;
I can myselven in this cas nat rede!
    WHAT shal I telle more her com-
    pleining?
    Hit is so long, hit were an hevy
    thing.
In her epistle Naso telleth al;
But shortly to the ende I telle shal.
The goddes have her holpen, for pitee;
And, in the signe of Taurus, men may see
The stones of her coroun shyne clere.
    I WOL no more speke of this matere;
    But thus this false lover can begyle
    His trewe love. The devil quyte him his
    whyle!
Explicit Legenda Adriane de Athenes.

INCIPIT LEGENDA PHILOMENE.

Deus dator formarum.

YIVER OF THE FORMES, THAT HAST wroght
The faire world, and bare hit in thy thoght
Eternally, or thou thy werk began,
Why madest thou, unto the slaundre of man,
Or, al be that hit was not thy doing,

As for that fyn to make swiche a thing,
Why suffrest thou that Tereus was bore,
That is in love so fals and so forswore,
That, fro this world up to the firste hevene,
Corrumpeth, whan that folk his name nevene?
And, as to me, so grisly was his dede,
That, whan that I his foule story rede,
Myn eyen wexen foule and sore also;
Yit last the venim of so longe ago,
That hit enfecteth him that wol beholde
The story of Tereus, of which I tolde.
Of Trace was he lord, and kin to Marte,
The cruel god that stant with blody darte;
And wedded had he, with a blisful chere,
King Pandiones faire doghter dere,
That highte Progne, flour of her contree,
Thogh Juno list nat at the feste be,
Ne Ymeneus, that god of wedding is;
But at the feste redy been, ywis,
The furies three, with alle hir mortel brond.
The owle al night aboute the balkes wond,
That prophet is of wo and of mischaunce.
This revel, ful of songe and ful of daunce,
Lasteth a fourtenight, or litel lasse.
But, shortly of this story for to passe,

Or by the fatal sustren had my dom,
So ny myn herte never thing me com
As thou, myn Ypermistra, doghter dere!
Tak heed what I thy fader sey thee here,
And werk after thy wyser evermo.
For alderfirste, doghter, I love thee so
That al the world to me nis half so leef;
Ne I nolde rede thee to thy mischeef
For al the gode under the colde mone;
And what I mene, hit shal be seid right sone,
With protestacioun, as in this wyse,
That, but thou do as I shal thee devyse,
Thou shalt be deed, by him that al hath wroght!
At shorte wordes, thou nescapest noght
Out of my paleys, or that thou be deed,
But thou consente and werke after my reed;
Tak this to thee for ful conclusioun.
THIS Ypermistra caste her eyen doun,
And quook as dooth the leef of aspe
grene;
Deed wex her hewe, and lyk as ash to sene,
And seyde: Lord and fader, al your wille,
After my might, God wot, I shal fulfille,
So hit to me be no confusioun.
I NIL, quod he, have noon excepcioun;
And out he caughte a knyf, as rasour
kene;

Hyd this, quod he, that hit be nat ysene;
And, whan thyn husbond is to bedde ygo,
Whyl that he slepeth, cut his throte atwo.
For in my dremes hit is warned me
How that my nevew shal my bane be,
But whiche I noot, wherfor I wol be siker.
Yif thou sey nay, we two shul have a biker
As I have seyd, by him that I have sworn.
THIS Ypermistra hath ny her wit for-
lorn;
And, for to passen harmles of that
place,
She graunted him; ther was non other grace.
And therwithal a costrel taketh he,
And seyde: Herof a draught, or two or three,
Yif him to drinke, whan he goth to reste,
And he shal slepe as longe as ever thee leste,
The narcotiks and opies been so stronge:
And go thy wey, lest that him thinke longe.
OUT comth the bryd, & with ful sober
chere,
As is of maidens ofte the manere,
To chambre is broght with revel and with
songe,
And shortly, lest this tale be to longe,
This Lino and she ben sone broght to bedde;
And every wight out at the dore him spedde.

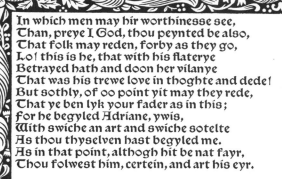

In which men may hir worthinesse see,
Than, preye I God, thou peynted be also,
That folk may reden, forby as they go,
Lo! this is he, that with his flaterye
Betrayed hath and doon her vilanye
That was his trewe love in thoghte and dede!
But sothly, of oo point yit may they rede,
That ye ben lyk your fader as in this;
For he begyled Adriane, ywis,
With swiche an art and swiche sotelte
As thou thyselven hast begyled me.
As in that point, althogh hit be nat fayr,
Thou folwest him, certein, and art his eyr.

But sin thus sinfully ye me begyle,
By body mote ye seen, within a whyle,
Right in the haven of Athenes fletinge,
Withouten sepulture and buryinge;
Thogh ye ben harder than is any stoon,
🖎 And, whan this lettre was forth sent anoon
And knew how brotel and how fals he was,
She for dispeyr fordide herself, allas!
Swich sorwe hath she, for she besette her so.
Be war, ye women, of your sotil fo,
Sin yit this day men may ensample see;
And trusteth, as in love, no man but me.
Explicit Legenda Phillis.

INCIPIT LEGENDA YPERMISTRE.

GRECE WHYLOM WEREN brethren two,
Of whiche that oon was called Danao,
That many a sone hath of his body wonne,
As swiche false lovers ofte conne.
Among his sones alle ther was oon
That aldermost he lovede of everichoon.
And whan this child was born, this Danao
Shoop him a name, and called him Lino.
That other brother called was Egiste,
That was of love as fals as ever him liste,
And many a doghter gat he in his lyve;
Of which he gat upon his righte wyve
A doghter dere, and dide her for to calle
Ypermistra, yongest of hem alle;
The whiche child, of her nativitee,
To alle gode thewes born was she,
As lyked to the goddes, or she was born,
That of the shefe she sholde be the corn;
The Wirdes, that we clepen Destinee,
Hath shapen her that she mot nedes be
Pitouse, sadde, wyse, and trewe as steel;
And to this woman hit accordeth weel.
For, though that Venus yaf her greet beautee,
With Jupiter compouned so was she
That conscience, trouthe, and dreed of shame,
And of her wyfhood for to kepe her name,
This, thoughte her, was felicitee as here.

And rede Mars was, that tyme of the yere,
So feble, that his malice is him raft,
Repressed hath Venus his cruel craft;
What with Venus and other oppressioun
Of houses, Mars his venim is adoun,
That Ypermistra dar nat handle a knyf
In malice, thogh she sholde lese her lyf.
But natheles, as heven gan tho turne,
To badde aspectes hath she of Saturne,
That made her for to deyen in prisoun,
As I shal after make mencioun.
O Danao and Egistes also,
Althogh so be that they were brethren two,
For thilke tyme nas spared no linage,
Hit lyked hem to maken mariage
Betwix Ypermistra and him Lino,
And casten swiche a day hit shal be so;
And ful acorded was hit witterly;
The array is wroght, the tyme is faste by.
And thus Lino hath of his fadres brother
The doghter wedded, and eche of hem hath other.
THE torches brennen & the lampes brighte,
The sacrifices been ful redy dighte;
Thencens out of the fyre reketh sote,
The flour, the leef is rent up by the rote
To maken garlands and corounes hye;
Ful is the place of soun of minstralcye,
Of songes amorous of mariage,
As thilke tyme was the pleyn usage.
And this was in the paleys of Egiste,
That in his hous was lord, right as him liste;
And thus the day they dryven to an ende;
The frendes taken leve, and hoom they wende.
The night is come, the bryd shal go to bedde;
Egiste to his chambre faste him spedde,
And privily he let his doghter calle.
Whan that the hous was voided of hem alle,
He loked on his doghter with glad chere,
And to her spak, as ye shul after here.
MY righte doghter, tresor of myn herte!
Sin first that day that shapen was my sherte,

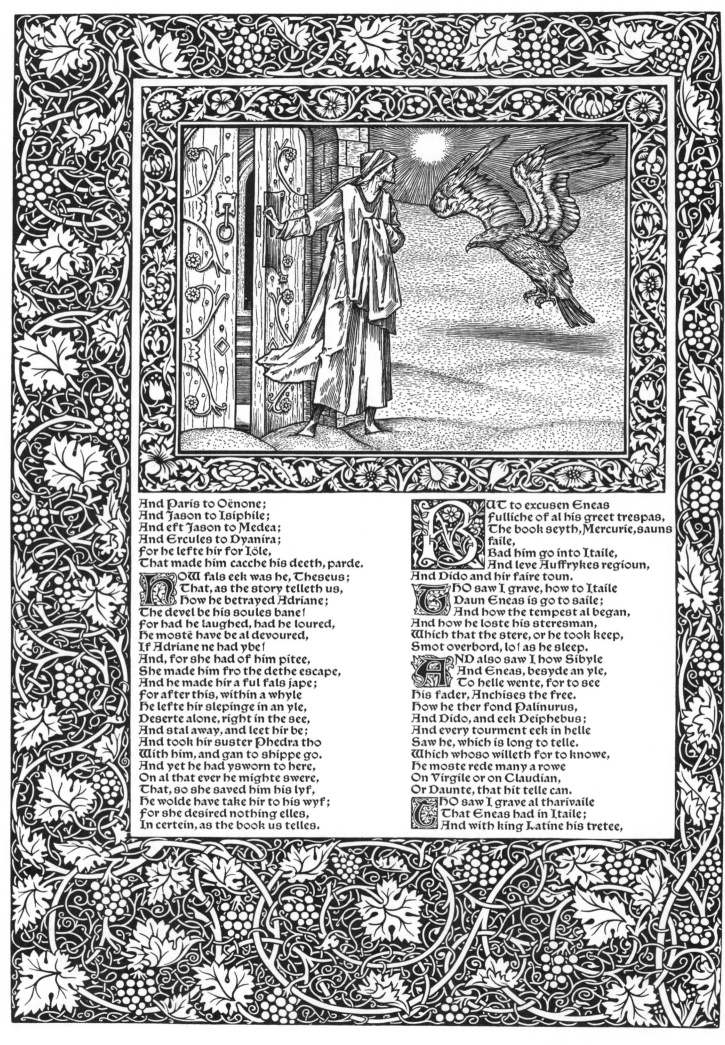

And Paris to Oënone;
And Jason to Isiphile;
And eft Jason to Medea;
And Ercules to Dyanira;
For he lefte hir for Iöle,
That made him cacche his deeth, parde.

NOW fals eek was he, Theseus;
That, as the story telleth us,
How he betrayed Adriane;
The devel be his soules bane!
For had he laughed, had he loured,
He mostë have be al devoured,
If Adriane ne had ybe!
And, for she had of him pitee,
She made him fro the dethe escape,
And he made hir a ful fals jape;
For after this, within a whyle
He lefte hir slepinge in an yle,
Deserte alone, right in the see,
And stal away, and leet hir be;
And took hir suster Phedra tho
With him, and gan to shippe go.
And yet he had ysworn to here,
On al that ever he mighte swere,
That, so she saved him his lyf,
He wolde have take hir to his wyf;
For she desired nothing elles,
In certein, as the book us telles.

BUT to excusen Eneas
Fulliche of al his greet trespas,
The book seyth, Mercurie, sauns
faile,
Bad him go into Itaile,
And leve Auffrykes regioun,
And Dido and hir faire toun.

THO saw I grave, how to Itaile
Daun Eneas is go to saile;
And how the tempest al began,
And how he loste his steresman,
Which that the stere, or he took keep,
Smot overbord, lo! as he sleep.

AND also saw I how Sibyle
And Eneas, besyde an yle,
To helle wente, for to see
His fader, Anchises the free.
How he ther fond Palinurus,
And Dido, and eek Deiphebus;
And every tourment eek in helle
Saw he, which is long to telle.
Which whoso willeth for to knowe,
He moste rede many a rowe
On Virgile or on Claudian,
Or Daunte, that hit telle can.

THO saw I grave al tharivaile
That Eneas had in Itaile;
And with king Latine his tretee,

And alle the batailles that he
Was at himself, and eek his knightes,
Or he had al ywonne his rightes;
And how he Turnus refte his lyf,
And wan Lavyna to his wyf;
And al the mervelous signals
Of the goddes celestials;
How, maugre Juno, Eneas,
For al hir sleighte and hir compas,
Acheved al his aventure;
For Jupiter took of him cure
At the prayere of Venus;
The whiche I preye alway save us,
And us ay of our sorwes lighte!

WHAN I had seyen al this sighte
In this noble temple thus,
A, Lord! thoughte I, that madest us,
Yet saw I never swich noblesse
Of images, ne swich richesse,
As I saw graven in this chirche;
But not woot I who dide hem wirche,
Ne wher I am, ne in what contree.
But now wol I go out and see,
Right at the wiket, if I can
See owher stering any man,
That may me telle wher I am.

WHEN I out at the dores cam,
I faste aboute me beheld.
Then saw I but a large feld,

As fer as that I mighte see,
Withouten toun, or hous, or tree,
Or bush, or gras, or ered lond;
For al the feld nas but of sond
As smal as man may see yet lye
In the desert of Libye;
Ne I no maner creature,
That is yformed by nature,
Ne saw, me for to rede or wisse.
O Crist, thoughte I, that art in blisse,
Fro fantom and illusioun
Me save! and with devocioun
Myn yën to the heven I caste.

THO was I war, lo! at the laste,
That faste by the sonne, as hyë
As kenne mighte I with myn yë,
Me thoughte I saw an egle sore,
But that hit semed moche more
Then I had any egle seyn.
But this as sooth as deeth, certeyn,
Hit was of golde, and shoon so brighte,
That never saw men such a sighte,
But if the heven hadde ywonne
Al newe of golde another sonne;
So shoon the egles fethres brighte,
And somwhat dounward gan hit lighte.
Explicit Liber Primus.

THE HOUS OF FAME ❦ LIBER SECUNDUS.

Incipit Liber Secundus ❦ Proem.

HERKNETH, EVERY MANER MAN
That English understonde can,
And listeth of my dreem to lere;
For now at erste shul ye here
So selly an avisioun,
That Isaye, ne Scipioun,
Ne king Nabugodonosor,
Pharo, Turnus, ne Elcanor,
Ne mette swich a dreem as this!
Now faire blisful, O Cipris,
So be my favour at this tyme!

And ye, me to endyte and ryme
Helpeth, that on Parnaso dwelle
By Elicon the clere welle.

O THOUGHT, that wroot al that I mette,
And in the tresorie hit shette
Of my brayn! now shal men see
If any vertu in thee be,
To tellen al my dreem aright;
Now kythe thyn engyn and might!
The Dream.

THIS egle, of which I
have yow told,
That shoon with feth-
res as of gold,
Which that so hyë gan
to sore,
I gan beholde more
and more,
To see hir beautee and
the wonder;
But never was ther dint of thonder,
Ne that thing that men calle foudre,
That smoot somtyme a tour to poudre,
And in his swifte coming brende,
That so swythe gan descende,
As this foul, whan hit behelde
That I aroume was in the felde;
And with his grimme pawes stronge,
Within his sharpe nayles longe,
Me, fleinge, at a swappe he hente,
And with his sours agayn up wente,

THE HOUS OF FAME · LIBER PRIMUS.

Incipit Liber Primus · Proem.

GOD TURNE US EVERY DREEM TO GODE!
For hit is wonder, by the rode,
To my wit, what causeth swevenes
Either on morwes, or on evenes;
And why the effect folweth of somme,
And of somme hit shal never come;

Why that is an avisioun,
And this a revelacioun;
Why this a dreem, why that a sweven,
And nat to every man liche even;
Why this a fantom, these oracles,
I noot; but whoso of these miracles
The causes knoweth bet than I,
Devyne he; for I certeinly
Ne can hem noght, ne never thinke
To besily my wit to swinke,
To knowe of hir signifiaunce
The gendres, neither the distaunce
Of tymes of hem, ne the causes
Forwhy this more than that cause is;
As if folkes complexiouns
Make hem dreme of reflexiouns;
Or elles thus, as other sayn,
For to greet feblenesse of brayn,
By abstinence, or by seeknesse,
Prison, stewe, or greet distresse;
Or elles by disordinaunce
Of naturel acustomaunce
That som man is to curious
In studie, or melancolious,
Or thus, so inly ful of drede,
That no man may him bote bede;

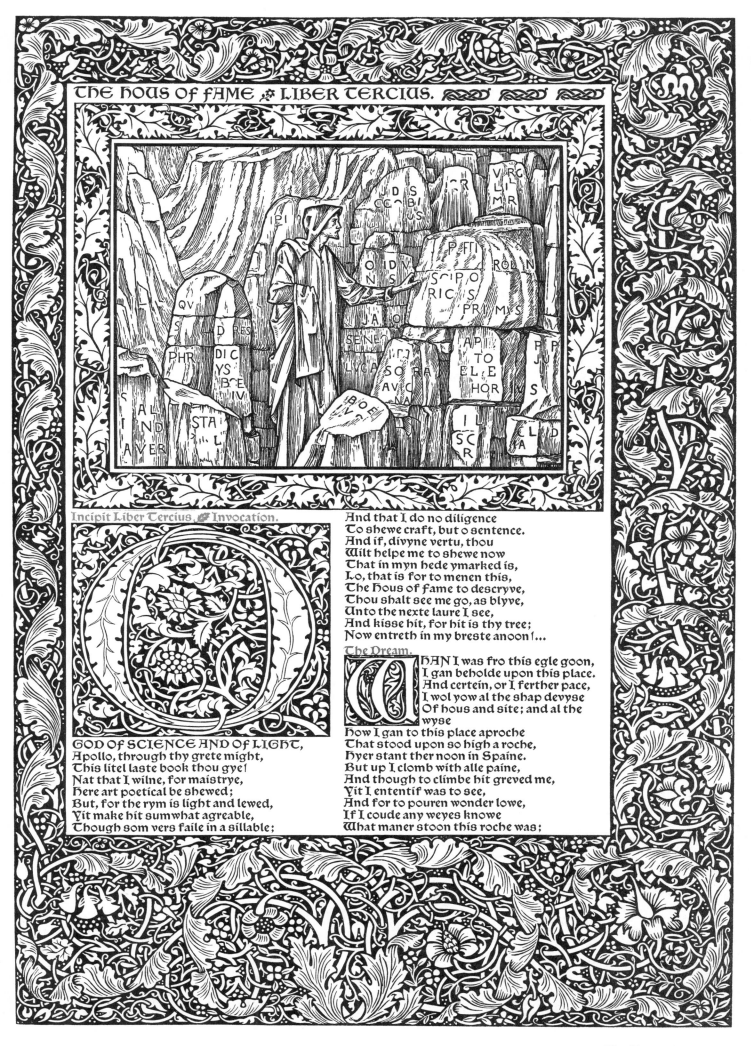

Incipit Liber Tercius. ❦ Invocation.

GOD OF SCIENCE AND OF LIGHT,
Apollo, through thy grete might,
This litel laste book thou gye!
Nat that I wilne, for maistrye,
Here art poetical be shewed;
But, for the rym is light and lewed,
Yit make hit sumwhat agreable,
Though som vers faile in a sillable;

And that I do no diligence
To shewe craft, but o sentence.
And if, divyne vertu, thou
Wilt helpe me to shewe now
That in myn hede ymarked is,
Lo, that is for to menen this,
The Hous of Fame to descryve,
Thou shalt see me go, as blyve,
Unto the nexte laure I see,
And kisse hit, for hit is thy tree;
Now entreth in my breste anoon!...

The Dream.

WHAN I was fro this egle goon,
I gan beholde upon this place.
And certein, or I ferther pace,
I wol yow al the shap devyse
Of hous and site; and al the wyse
How I gan to this place aproche
That stood upon so high a roche,
Hyer stant ther noon in Spaine.
But up I clomb with alle paine,
And though to climbe hit greved me,
Yit I ententif was to see,
And for to pouren wonder lowe,
If I coude any weyes knowe
What maner stoon this roche was;

Me carÿinge in his clawes starke
As lightly as I were a larke,
How high, I can not telle yow,
for I cam up, I niste how.
for so astonied and asweved
Was every vertu in my heved,
What with his sours and with my drede,
That al my feling gan to dede;
forwhy hit was to greet affray.
THUS I longe in his clawes lay,
Til at the laste he to me spak
In mannes vois, and seyde: Awak!
And be not so agast, for shame!
And called me tho by my name.
And, for I sholde the bet abreyde,
Me mette, Awak, to me he seyde,
Right in the same vois and stevene
That useth oon I coude nevene;
And with that vois, soth for to sayn,
My minde cam to me agayn;
for hit was goodly seyd to me,
So nas hit never wont to be.
AND herwithal I gan to stere,
And he me in his feet to bere,
Til that he felte that I had hete,
And felte eek tho myn herte bete.
And tho gan he me to disporte,
And with wordes to comforte,

And sayde twyës: Seynte Marie!
Thou art noyous for to carie,
And nothing nedeth hit, parde!
for also wis God helpe me
As thou non harm shalt have of this;
And this cas, that betid thee is,
Is for thy lore and for thy prow;
Let see! darst thou yet loke now?
Be ful assured, boldely,
I am thy frend. And therwith I
Gan for to wondren in my minde.
O God, thoughte I, that madest kinde,
Shal I non other weyes dye?
Wher Joves wol me stellifye,
Or what thing may this signifye?
I neither am Enok, ne Elye,
Ne Romulus, ne Ganymede
That was ybore up, as men rede,
To hevene with dan Jupiter,
And maad the goddes boteler.
LO! this was tho my fantasye!
But he that bar me gan espye
That I so thoghte, and seyde this:
Thou demest of thyself amis;
for Joves is not theraboute,
I dar wel putte thee out of doute,
To make of thee as yet a sterre.
But er I bere thee moche ferre,

And loveth him, the which that right for love
Upon a cros, our soules for to beye,
First starf, and roos, and sit in hevene above;
For he nil falsen no wight, dar I seye,
That wol his herte al hoolly on him leye.
And sin he best to love is, and most meke,
What nedeth feyned loves for to seke?

Lo here, of Payens corsed olde rytes,
Lo here, what alle hir goddes may availle;
Lo here, these wrecched worldes appetytes;
Lo here, the fyn and guerdon for travaille
Of Jove, Appollo, of Mars of swich rascaille!
Lo here, the forme of olde clerkes speche
In poetrye, if ye hir bokes seche.

O moral Gower, this book I directe

To thee, and to the philosophical Strode,
To vouchen sauf, ther nede is, to corecte,
Of your benignitees and zeles gode.
And to that sothfast Crist, that starf on rode,
With al myn herte of mercy ever I preye;
And to the Lord right thus I speke and seye:

Thou oon, and two, and three, eterne on lyve,
That regnest ay in three and two and oon,
Uncircumscript, and al mayst circumscryve,
Us from visible and invisible foon
Defende; and to thy mercy, everichoon,
So make us, Jesus, for thy grace digne,
For love of mayde and moder thyn benigne!
Amen.
Explicit Liber Troili et Criseydis.

Kelmscott

That every wight gan on hem shoute,
And for to laughe as they were wode;
Such game fonde they in hir hode.
THO com another companye,
That had ydoon the traiterye,
The harm, the gretest wikkednesse
That any herte couthe gesse;
And preyed hir to han good fame,
And that she nolde hem doon no shame,
But yeve hem loos and good renoun,
And do hit blowe in clarioun.
Nay, wis! quod she, hit were a vyce;
Al be ther in me no justyce,
Me listeth not to do hit now,
Ne this nil I not graunte yow.
THO come ther lepinge in a route,
And gonne choppen al aboute
Every man upon the croune,
That al the halle gan to soune,
And seyden: Lady, lefe and dere,
We ben swich folk as ye mowe here.
To tellen al the tale aright,
We ben shrewes, every wight,
And han delyt in wikkednes,
As gode folk han in goodnes;
And joye to be knowen shrewes,
And fulle of vyce and wikked thewes;

Wherfor we preyen yow, a-rowe,
That our fame swich be knowe
In alle thing right as hit is.
I GRAUNTE hit yow, quod she, ywis.
But what art thou that seyst this tale,
That werest on thy hose a pale,
And on thy tipet swiche a belle!
Madame, quod he, sooth to telle,
I am that ilke shrewe, ywis,
That brende the temple of Isidis
In Athenes, lo, that citee.
And wherfor didest thou so? quod she.
By my thrift, quod he, madame,
I wolde fayn han had a fame,
As other folk hadde in the toun,
Althogh they were of greet renoun
For hir vertu and for hir thewes;
Thoughte I, as greet a fame han shrewes,
Thogh hit be but for shrewednesse,
As gode folk han for goodnesse;
And sith I may not have that oon,
That other nil I noght forgoon.
And for to gette of fames hyre,
The temple sette I al afyre.
Now do our loos be blowen swythe,
As wisly be thou ever blythe.
Gladly, quod she; thou Eolus,

Herestow not what they preyen us?
  Madame, yis, ful wel, quod he,
And I wil trumpen hit, pardé!
  And tok his blakke trumpe faste,
And gan to puffen and to blaste,
Til hit was at the worldes ende.
  WITH that I gan aboute wende;
for oon that stood right at my bak,
Me thoughte, goodly to me spak,
And seyde: frend, what is thy name?
Artow come hider to han fame?
  Nay, forsothe, frend! quod I;
I cam noght hider, graunt mercy!
for no swich cause, by my heed!
Suffyceth me, as I were deed,
That no wight have my name in honde.
I woot myself best how I stonde;
for what I drye or what I thinke,
I wol myselven al hit drinke,
Certeyn, for the more part,
As ferforth as I can myn art.
  But what dost thou here than? quod he.
  Quod I: That wol I tellen thee,
The cause why I stonde here:
Som newe tydings for to lere:
Som newe thinges, I not what,
Tydinges, other this or that,

Of love, or swiche thinges glade.
for certeynly, he that me made
To comen hider, seyde me,
I shulde bothe here and see,
In this place, wonder thinges;
But these be no swiche tydinges
As I mene of No? quod he.
  And I answerde: No, pardee!
for wel I wiste, ever yit,
Sith that first I hadde wit,
That som folk han desyred fame
Dyversly, and loos, and name;
But certeynly, I niste how
Ne wher that fame dwelte, er now;
Ne eek of hir descripcioun,
Ne also hir condicioun,
Ne the ordre of hir dome,
Unto the tyme I hider come.
  Whiche be, lo, these tydinges,
That thou now thus hider bringes,
That thou hast herd? quod he to me;
But now, no fors; for wel I see
What thou desyrest for to here.
Com forth, and stond no longer here,
And I wol thee, withouten drede,
In swich another place lede,
Ther thou shalt here many oon.

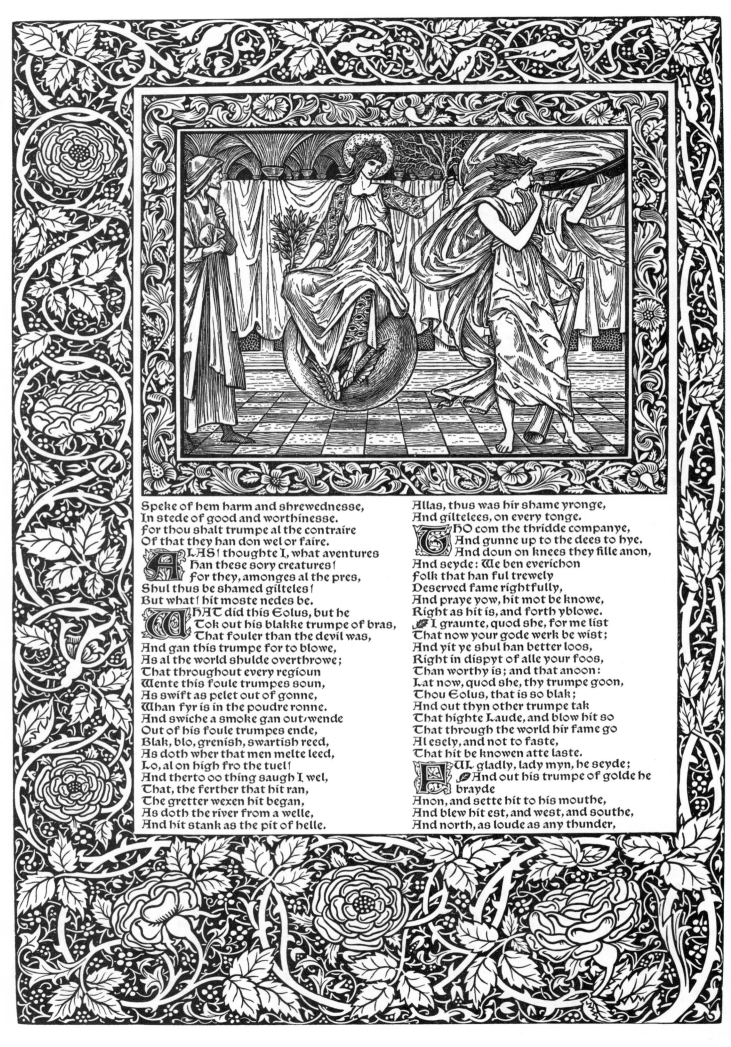

Speke of hem harm and shrewednesse,
In stede of good and worthinesse.
For thou shalt trumpe al the contraire
Of that they han don wel or faire.
ALAS! thoughte I, what aventures
Han these sory creatures!
For they, amonges al the pres,
Shul thus be shamed gilteles!
But what! hit moste nedes be.
WHAT did this Eolus, but he
Tok out his blakke trumpe of bras,
That fouler than the devil was,
And gan this trumpe for to blowe,
As al the world shulde overthrowe;
That throughout every regioun
Wente this foule trumpes soun,
As swift as pelet out of gonne,
Whan fyr is in the poudre ronne.
And swiche a smoke gan out-wende
Out of his foule trumpes ende,
Blak, blo, grenish, swartish reed,
As doth wher that men melte leed,
Lo, al on high fro the tuel!
And therto oo thing saugh I wel,
That, the ferther that hit ran,
The gretter wexen hit began,
As doth the river from a welle,
And hit stank as the pit of helle.

Allas, thus was hir shame yronge,
And giltelees, on every tonge.
THO com the thridde companye,
And gunne up to the dees to hye.
And doun on knees they fille anon,
And seyde: We ben everichon
Folk that han ful trewely
Deserved fame rightfully,
And praye yow, hit mot be knowe,
Right as hit is, and forth yblowe.
I graunte, quod she, for me list
That now your gode werk be wist;
And yit ye shul han better loos,
Right in dispyt of alle your foos,
Than worthy is; and that anoon:
Lat now, quod she, thy trumpe goon,
Thou Eolus, that is so blak;
And out thyn other trumpe tak
That highte Laude, and blow hit so
That through the world hir fame go
Al esely, and not to faste,
That hit be knowen atte laste.
FUL gladly, lady myn, he seyde;
And out his trumpe of golde he
brayde
Anon, and sette hit to his mouthe,
And blew hit est, and west, and southe,
And north, as loude as any thunder,

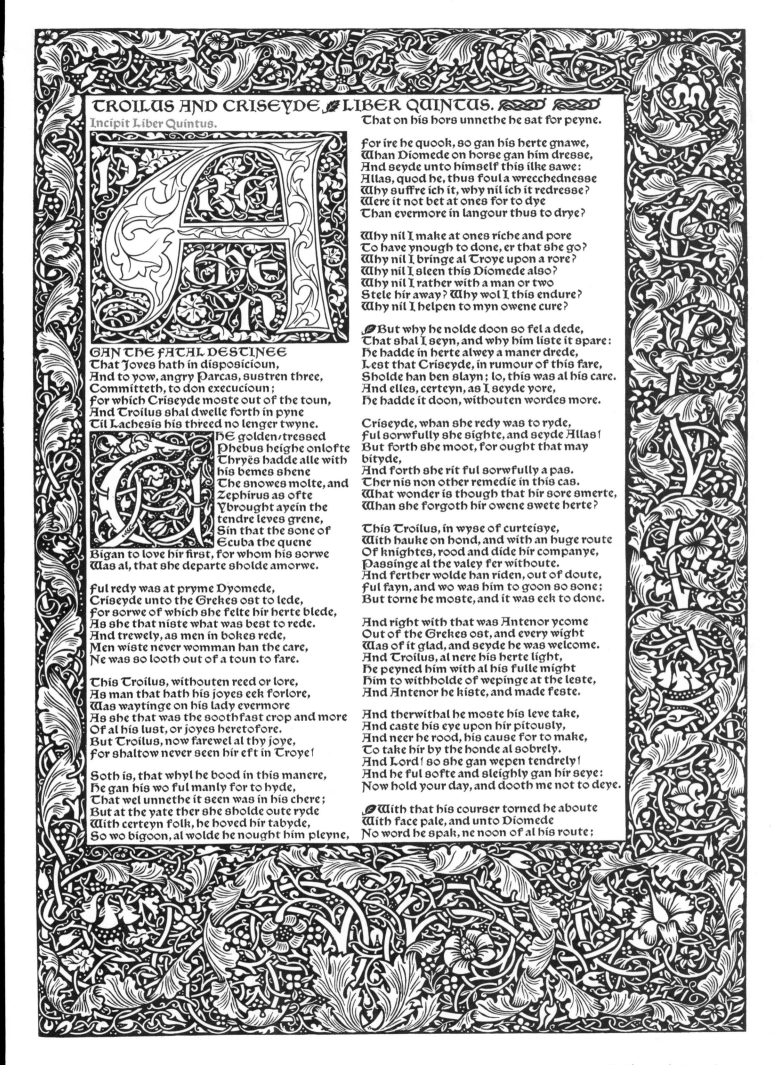

TROILUS AND CRISEYDE. LIBER QUINTUS.

Incipit Liber Quintus.

A

GAN THE FATAL DESTINEE
That Joves hath in disposicioun,
And to yow, angry Parcas, sustren three,
Committeth, to don execucioun;
For which Criseyde moste out of the toun,
And Troilus shal dwelle forth in pyne
Til Lachesis his threed no lenger twyne.

THE golden-tressed
Phebus heighe onlofte
Thryës hadde alle with
his bemes shene
The snowes molte, and
Zephirus as ofte
Ybrought ayein the
tendre leves grene,
Sin that the sone of
Ecuba the quene
Bigan to love hir first, for whom his sorwe
Was al, that she departe sholde amorwe.

Ful redy was at pryme Dyomede,
Criseyde unto the Grekes ost to lede,
For sorwe of which she felte hir herte blede,
As she that niste what was best to rede.
And trewely, as men in bokes rede,
Men wiste never womman han the care,
Ne was so looth out of a toun to fare.

This Troilus, withouten reed or lore,
As man that hath his joyes eek forlore,
Was waytinge on his lady evermore
As she that was the soothfast crop and more
Of al his lust, or joyes heretofore.
But Troilus, now farewel al thy joye,
For shaltow never seen hir eft in Troye!

Soth is, that whyl he bood in this manere,
He gan his wo ful manly for to hyde,
That wel unnethe it seen was in his chere;
But at the yate ther she sholde oute ryde
With certeyn folk, he hoved hir tabyde,
So wo bigoon, al wolde he nought him pleyne,

That on his hors unnethe he sat for peyne.

For ire he quook, so gan his herte gnawe,
Whan Diomede on horse gan him dresse,
And seyde unto himself this ilke sawe:
Allas, quod he, thus foul a wrecchednesse
Why suffre ich it, why nil ich it redresse?
Were it not bet at ones for to dye
Than evermore in langour thus to drye?

Why nil I make at ones riche and pore
To have ynough to done, er that she go?
Why nil I bringe al Troye upon a rore?
Why nil I sleen this Diomede also?
Why nil I rather with a man or two
Stele hir away? Why wol I this endure?
Why nil I helpen to myn owene cure?

But why he nolde doon so fel a dede,
That shal I seyn, and why him liste it spare:
He hadde in herte alwey a maner drede,
Lest that Criseyde, in rumour of this fare,
Sholde han ben slayn; lo, this was al his care.
And elles, certeyn, as I seyde yore,
He hadde it doon, withouten wordes more.

Criseyde, whan she redy was to ryde,
Ful sorwfully she sighte, and seyde Allas!
But forth she moot, for ought that may bityde,
And forth she rit ful sorwfully a pas.
Ther nis non other remedie in this cas.
What wonder is though that hir sore smerte,
Whan she forgoth hir owene swete herte?

This Troilus, in wyse of curteisye,
With hauke on hond, and with an huge route
Of knightes, rood and dide hir companye,
Passinge al the valey fer withoute.
And ferther wolde han riden, out of doute,
Ful fayn, and wo was him to goon so sone;
But torne he moste, and it was eek to done.

And right with that was Antenor ycome
Out of the Grekes ost, and every wight
Was of it glad, and seyde he was welcome.
And Troilus, al nere his herte light,
He peyned him with al his fulle might
Him to withholde of wepinge at the leste,
And Antenor he kiste, and made feste.

And therwithal he moste his leve take,
And caste his eye upon hir pitously,
And neer he rood, his cause for to make,
To take hir by the honde al sobrely.
And Lord! so she gan wepen tendrely!
And he ful softe and sleighly gan hir seye:
Now hold your day, and dooth me not to deye.

With that his courser torned he aboute
With face pale, and unto Diomede
No word he spak, ne noon of al his route;

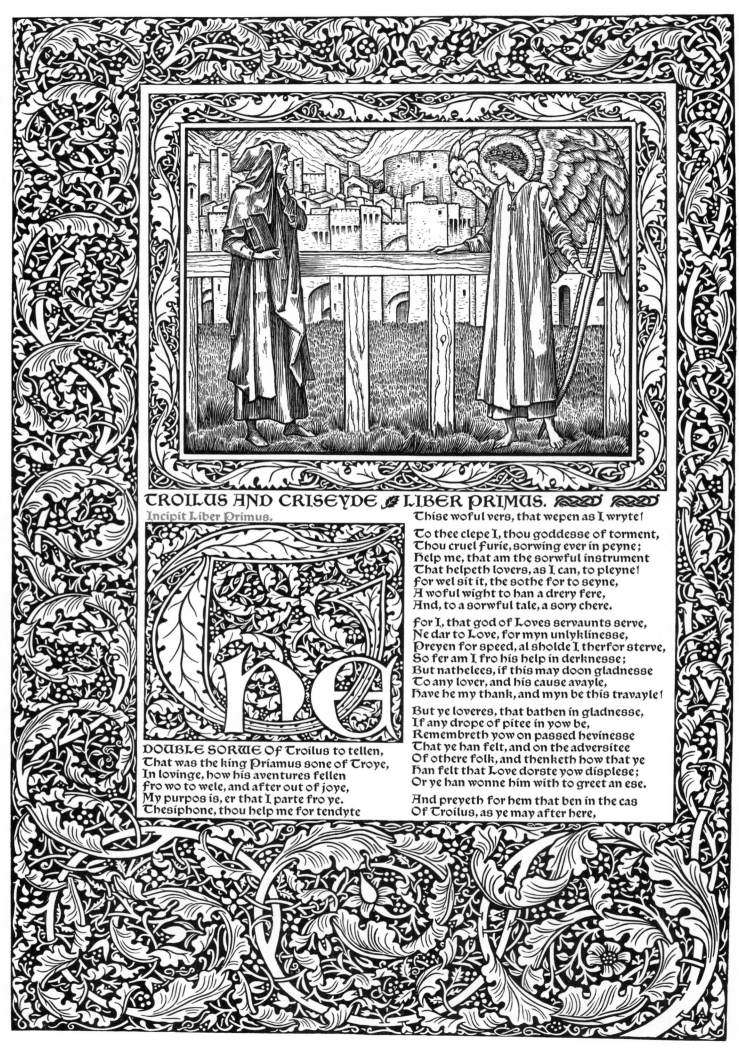

TROILUS AND CRISEYDE ✿ LIBER PRIMUS.

Incipit Liber Primus.

Thise woful vers, that wepen as I wryte!

To thee clepe I, thou goddesse of torment,
Thou cruel Furie, sorwing ever in peyne;
Help me, that am the sorwful instrument
That helpeth lovers, as I can, to pleyne!
for wel sit it, the sothe for to seyne,
A woful wight to han a drery fere,
And, to a sorwful tale, a sory chere.

for I, that god of Loves servaunts serve,
Ne dar to Love, for myn unlyklinesse,
Preyen for speed, al sholde I therfor sterve,
So fer am I fro his help in derknesse;
But natheles, if this may doon gladnesse
To any lover, and his cause avayle,
Have he my thank, and myn be this travayle!

But ye loveres, that bathen in gladnesse,
If any drope of pitee in yow be,
Remembreth yow on passed hevinesse
That ye han felt, and on the adversitee
Of othere folk, and thenketh how that ye
Han felt that Love dorste yow displese;
Or ye han wonne him with to greet an ese.

And preyeth for hem that ben in the cas
Of Troilus, as ye may after here,

THE DOUBLE SORWE Of Troilus to tellen,
That was the king Priamus sone of Troye,
In lovinge, how his aventures fellen
fro wo to wele, and after out of joye,
My purpos is, er that I parte fro ye.
Thesiphone, thou help me for tendyte

That love hem bringe in hevene to solas,
And eek for me preyeth to God so dere,
That I have might to shewe, in som manere,
Swich peyne and wo as Loves folk endure,
In Troilus unsely aventure.

And biddeth eek for hem that been despeyred
In love, that never nil recovered be,
And eek for hem that falsly been apeyred
Thorugh wikked tonges, be it he or she;
Thus biddeth God, for his benignitee,
To graunte hem sone out of this world to pace,
That been despeyred out of Loves grace.

And biddeth eek for hem that been at ese,
That God hem graunte ay good per-
severaunce,
And sende hem might hir ladies so to plese,
That it to Love be worship and plesaunce.
For so hope I my soule best avaunce,
To preye for hem that Loves servaunts be,
And wryte hir wo, and live in charitee.

And for to have of hem compassioun
As though I were hir owene brother dere.
Now herkeneth with a gode entencioun,
For now wol I gon streight to my matere,
In whiche ye may the double sorwes here

Of Troilus, in loving of Criseyde,
And how that she forsook him er she deyde.

I T is wel wist, how that the
Grekes stronge
In armes with a thousand
shippes wente
To Troyewardes, and the citee
longe
Assegeden neigh ten yeer er
they stente,
And, in diverse wyse and oon
entente,
The ravisshing to wreken of
Eleyne,
By Paris doon, they wrought-
en al hir peyne.
Now fil it so, that in the toun
ther was
Dwellinge a lord of greet auc-
toritee,
A gret devyn that cleped was
Calkas,
That in science so expert was, that he
Knew wel that Troye sholde destroyed be,
By answere of his god, that highte thus,
Daun Phebus or Apollo Delphicus.

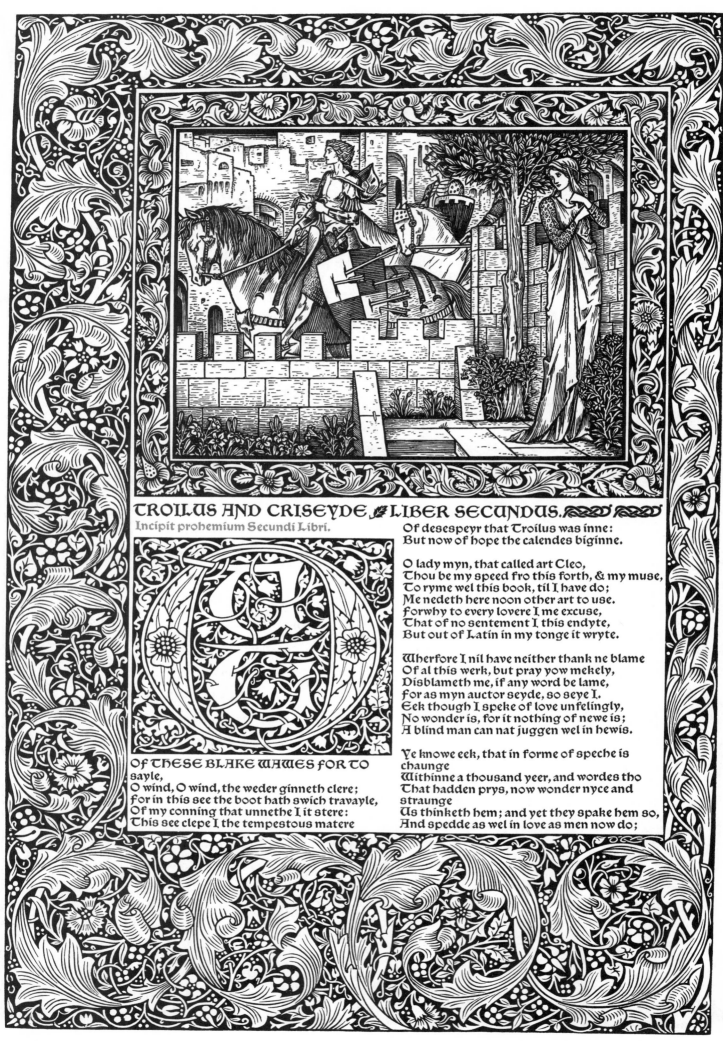

TROILUS AND CRISEYDE. LIBER SECUNDUS.

Incipit prohemium Secundi Libri.

Of desespeyr that Troilus was inne:
But now of hope the calendes biginne.

O lady myn, that called art Cleo,
Thou be my speed fro this forth, & my muse,
To ryme wel this book, til I have do;
Me nedeth here noon other art to use.
Forwhy to every lovere I me excuse,
That of no sentement I this endyte,
But out of Latin in my tonge it wryte.

Wherfore I nil have neither thank ne blame
Of al this werk, but pray yow mekely,
Disblameth me, if any word be lame,
For as myn auctor seyde, so seye I.
Eek though I speke of love unfelingly,
No wonder is, for it nothing of newe is;
A blind man can nat juggen wel in hewis.

Ye knowe eek, that in forme of speche is
chaunge
Withinne a thousand yeer, and wordes tho
That hadden prys, now wonder nyce and
straunge
Us thinketh hem; and yet they spake hem so,
And spedde as wel in love as men now do;

OF THESE BLAKE WAWES FOR TO
sayle,
O wind, O wind, the weder ginneth clere;
For in this see the boot hath swich travayle,
Of my conning that unnethe I it stere:
This see clepe I the tempestous matere

Eek for to winne love in sondry ages,
In sondry londes, sondry ben usages.

And forthy if it happe in any wyse,
That here be any lovere in this place
That herkeneth, as the story wol devyse,
How Troilus com to his lady grace,
And thenketh, so nolde I nat love purchace,
Or wondreth on his speche and his doinge,
I noot; but it is me no wonderinge;

For every wight which that to Rome went,
Halt nat o path, or alwey o manere;
Eek in some lond were al the gamen shent,
If that they ferde in love as men don here,
As thus, in open doing or in chere,
In visitinge, in forme, or seyde hir sawes;
Forthy men seyn, ech contree hath his lawes.

Eek scarsly been ther in this place three
That han in love seyd lyk and doon in al;
For to thy purpos this may lyken thee,
And thee right nought, yet al is seyd or shal;
Eek some men grave in tree, som in stoon
wal,
As it bitit; but sin I have begonne,
Myn auctor shal I folwen, if I conne.
Explicit prohemium Secundi Libri.

Incipit Liber Secundus.

IN May, that moder is of
monthes glade,
That fresshe floures,
blewe, and whyte, and
rede,
Ben quike agayn, that
winter dede made,
And ful of bawme is
fletinge every mede;
Whan Phebus doth his
brighte bemes sprede
Right in the whyte Bole, it so bitidde
As I shal singe, on Mayes day the thridde,

That Pandarus, for al his wyse speche,
Felte eek his part of loves shottes kene,
That, coude he never so wel of loving preche,
It made his hewe aday ful ofte grene;
So shoop it, that him fil that day a tene
In love, for which in wo to bedde he wente,
And made, er it was day, ful many a wente.

The swalwe Proignè, with a sorwful lay,
Whan morwe com, gan make hir weymentinge,
Why she forshapen was; and ever lay
Pandare abedde, half in a slomeringe,
Til she so neigh him made hir chiteringe

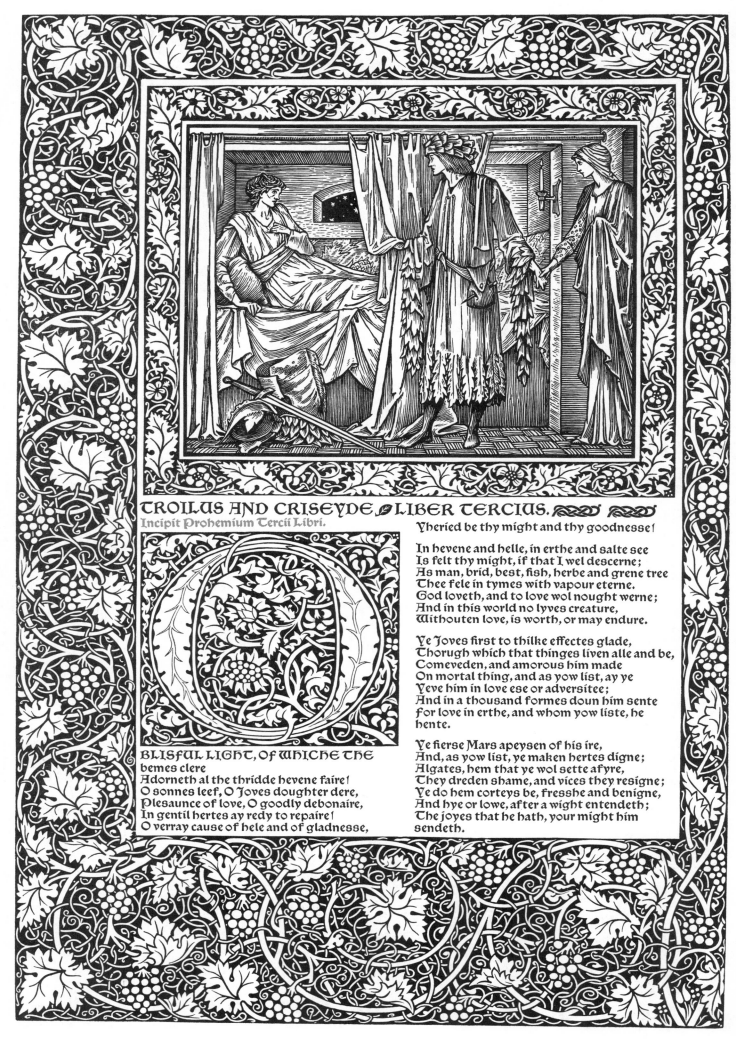

TROILUS AND CRISEYDE ❧ LIBER TERCIUS. ⤳⤳

Incipit Prohemium Tercii Libri.

Yheried be thy might and thy goodnesse!

In hevene and helle, in erthe and salte see
Is felt thy might, if that I wel descerne;
As man, brid, best, fish, herbe and grene tree
Thee fele in tymes with vapour eterne.
God loveth, and to love wol nought werne;
And in this world no lyves creature,
Withouten love, is worth, or may endure.

Ye Joves first to thilke effectes glade,
Thorugh which that thinges liven alle and be,
Comeveden, and amorous him made
On mortal thing, and as yow list, ay ye
Yeve him in love ese or adversitee;
And in a thousand formes doun him sente
For love in erthe, and whom yow liste, he
hente.

Ye fierse Mars apeysen of his ire,
And, as yow list, ye maken hertes digne;
Algates, hem that ye wol sette afyre,
They dreden shame, and vices they resigne;
Ye do hem corteys be, fresshe and benigne,
And hye or lowe, after a wight entendeth;
The joyes that he hath, your might him
sendeth.

BLISFUL LIGHT, OF WHICHE THE
bemes clere
Adorneth al the thridde hevene faire!
O sonnes leef, O Joves doughter dere,
Plesaunce of love, O goodly debonaire,
In gentil hertes ay redy to repaire!
O verray cause of hele and of gladnesse,

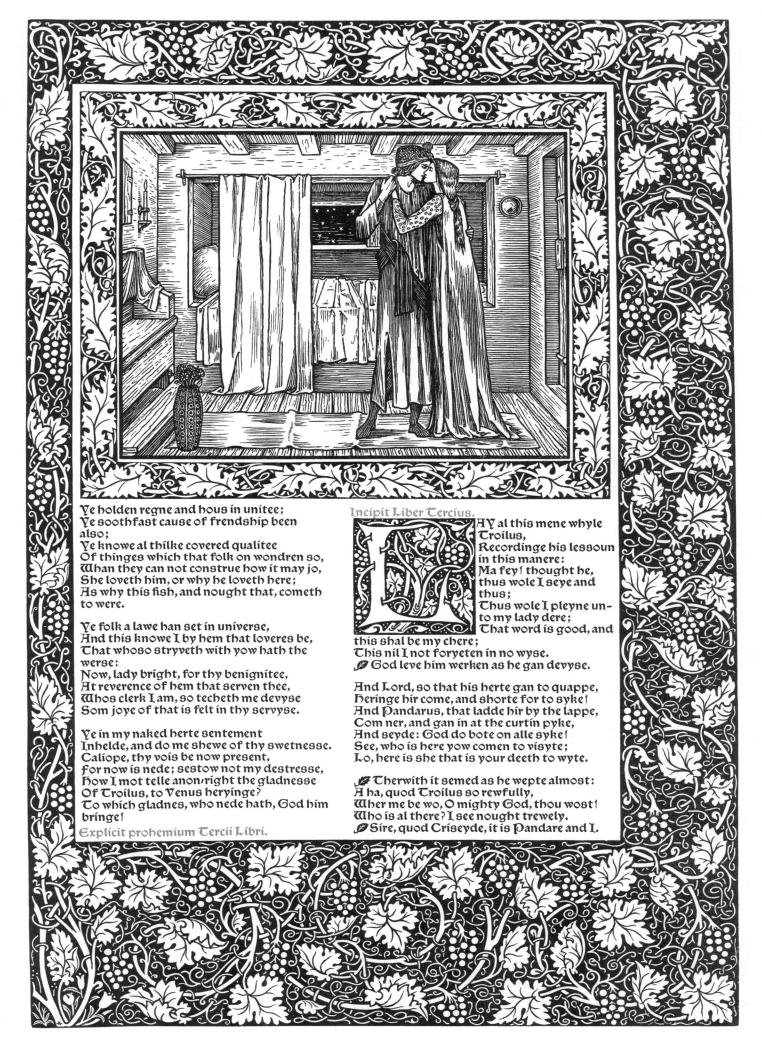

Ye holden regne and hous in unitee;
Ye soothfast cause of frendship been
also;
Ye knowe al thilke covered qualitee
Of thinges which that folk on wondren so,
Whan they can not construe how it may jo,
She loveth him, or why he loveth here;
As why this fish, and nought that, cometh
to were.

Ye folk a lawe han set in universe,
And this knowe I by hem that loveres be,
That whoso stryveth with yow hath the
werse:
Now, lady bright, for thy benignitee,
At reverence of hem that serven thee,
Whos clerk I am, so techeth me devyse
Som joye of that is felt in thy servyse.

Ye in my naked herte sentement
Inhelde, and do me shewe of thy swetnesse.
Caliope, thy vois be now present,
for now is nede; sestow not my destresse,
How I mot telle anon, right the gladnesse
Of Troilus, to Venus heryinge?
To which gladnes, who nede hath, God him
bringe!

Explicit prohemium Tercii Libri.

Incipit Liber Tercius.

LAY al this mene whyle
Troilus,
Recordinge his lessoun
in this manere:
Ma fey! thought he,
thus wole I seye and
thus;
Thus wole I pleyne un-
to my lady dere;
That word is good, and
this shal be my chere;
This nil I not foryeten in no wyse.
God leve him werken as he gan devyse.

And Lord, so that his herte gan to quappe,
Heringe hir come, and shorte for to syke!
And Pandarus, that ladde hir by the lappe,
Com ner, and gan in at the curtin pyke,
And seyde: God do bote on alle syke!
See, who is here yow comen to visyte;
Lo, here is she that is your deeth to wyte.

Therwith it semed as he wepte almost:
A ha, quod Troilus so rewfully,
Wher me be wo, O mighty God, thou wost!
Who is al there? I see nought trewely.
Sire, quod Criseyde, it is Pandare and I.

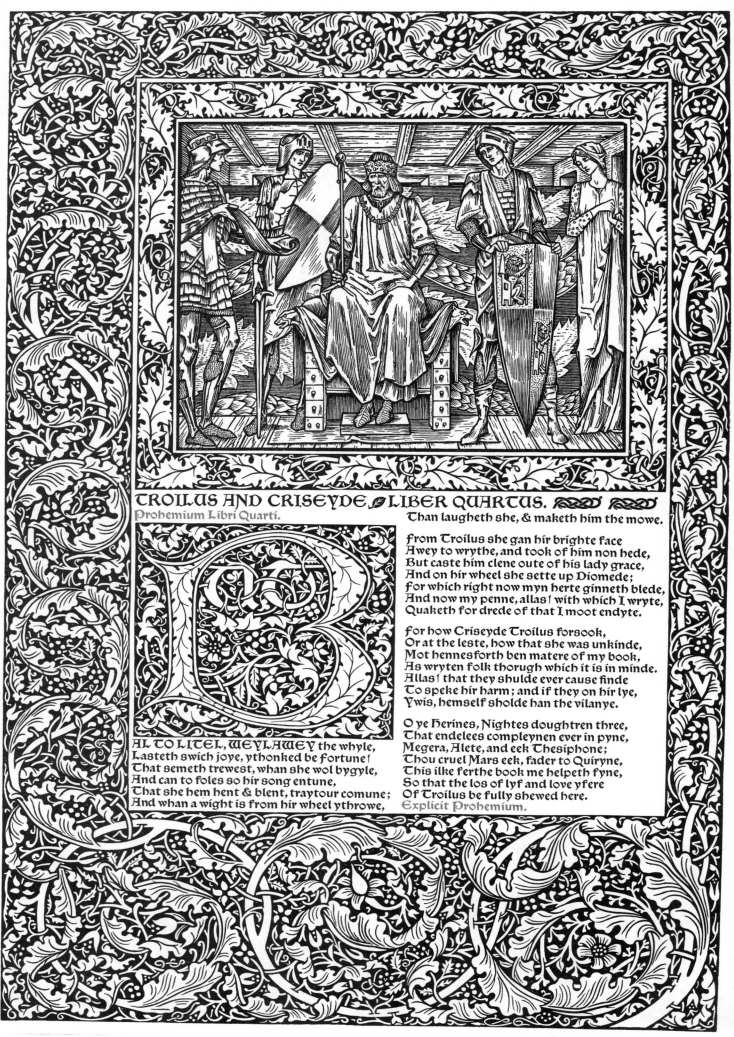

TROILUS AND CRISEYDE ☙ LIBER QUARTUS.

Prohemium Libri Quarti.

Than laugheth she, & maketh him the mowe.

from Troilus she gan hir brighte face
Awey to wrythe, and took of him non hede,
But caste him clene oute of his lady grace,
And on hir wheel she sette up Diomede;
for which right now myn herte ginneth blede,
And now my penne, allas! with which I wryte,
Quaketh for drede of that I moot endyte.

for how Criseyde Troilus forsook,
Or at the leste, how that she was unkinde,
Mot hennesforth ben matere of my book,
As wryten folk thorugh which it is in minde.
Allas! that they shulde ever cause finde
To speke hir harm; and if they on hir lye,
Ywis, hemself sholde han the vilanye.

O ye Herines, Nightes doughtren three,
That endelees compleynen ever in pyne,
Megera, Alete, and eek Thesiphone;
Thou cruel Mars eek, fader to Quiryne,
This ilke ferthe book me helpeth fyne,
So that the los of lyf and love yfere
Of Troilus be fully shewed here.
Explicit Prohemium.

B AL TO LITEL, WEYLAWEY the whyle,
Lasteth swich joye, ythonked be fortune!
That semeth trewest, whan she wol bygyle,
And can to foles so hir song entune,
That she hem hent & blent, traytour comune;
And whan a wight is from hir wheel ythrowe,

Incipit Quartus Liber.

LIGGINGE in ost, as I
have seyd er this,
The Grekes stronge,
aboute Troye toun,
Bifel that, whan that
Phebus shyning is
Upon the brest of Her-
cules Lyoun,
That Ector, with ful
many a bold baroun,
Caste on a day with Grekes for to fighte,
As he was wont to greve hem what he mighte.

Not I how longe or short it was bitwene
This purpos and that day they fighte mente;
But on a day wel armed, bright and shene,
Ector, and many a worthy wight out wente,
With spere in hond and bigge bowes bente;
And in the herd, withoute lenger lette,
Hir fomen in the feld anoon hem mette.

The longe day, with speres sharpe ygrounde,
With arwes, dartes, swerdes, maces felle,
They fighte and bringen hors and man to
grounde,
And with hir axes out the braynes quelle.

But in the laste shour, sooth for to telle,
The folk of Troye hemselven so misledden,
That with the worse at night homward they
fledden.

At whiche day was taken Antenor,
Maugre Polydamas or Monesteo,
Santippe, Sarpedon, Polynestor,
Polyte, or eek the Troian daun Ripheo,
And othere lasse folk, as Phebuseo.
So that, for harm, that day the folk of Troye
Dredden to lese a greet part of hir joye.

Of Pryamus was yeve, at Greek requeste,
A tyme of trewe, and tho they gonnen trete,
Hir prisoneres to chaungen, moste and leste,
And for the surplus yeven sommes grete.
This thing anoon was couth in every strete,
Bothe in thassege, in toune, and everywhere,
And with the firste it cam to Calkas ere.

Whan Calkas knew this tretis sholde holde,
In consistorie, among the Grekes, sone
He gan in thringe forth, with lordes olde,
And sette him thereas he was wont to done;
And with a chaunged face hem bad a bone,
For love of God, to don that reverence,

Of which the sone of Tydeus took hede,
As he that coude more than the crede
In swich a craft, and by the reyne hir hente;
And Troilus to Troye homward he wente.

This Diomede, that ladde hir by the brydel,
Whan that he saw the folk of Troye aweye,
Thoughte: Al my labour shal not been on ydel,
If that I may, for somwhat shal I seye.
For at the worste it may yet shorte our weye.
I have herd seyd, eek tymes twyës twelve:
He is a fool that wol foryete himselve.

But natheles this thoughte he wel ynough:
That certaynly I am aboute nought
If that I speke of love, or make it tough;
For douteles, if she have in hir thought
Him that I gesse, he may not been ybrought
So sone awey; but I shal finde a mene,
That she not wite as yet shal what I mene.

This Diomede, as he that coude his good,
Whan this was doon, gan fallen forth in speche
Of this and that, and asked why she stood
In swich disese, and gan hir eek biseche,
That if that he encrese mighte or eche
With any thing hir ese, that she sholde

Comaunde it him, and seyde he doon it wolde.

For trewely he swoor hir, as a knight,
That ther nas thing with whiche he mighte hir plese,
That he nolde doon his peyne & al his might
To doon it, for to doon hir herte an ese.
And preyede hir, she wolde hir sorwe apese,
And seyde: Ywis, we Grekes con have joye
To honouren yow, as wel as folk of Troye.

He seyde eek thus: I woot, yow thinketh straunge,
No wonder is, for it is to yow newe,
Thaqueintaunce of these Troianes to chaunge,
For folk of Grece, that ye never knewe.
But wolde never God but if as trewe
A Greek ye shulde among us alle finde
As any Troian is, and eek as kinde.

And by the cause I swoor yow right, lo, now,
To been your freend, and helply, to my might,
And for that more acqueintaunce eek of yow
Have ich had than another straunger wight,
So fro this forth I pray yow, day and night,
Comaundeth me, how sore that me smerte,
To doon al that may lyke unto your herte:

And that ye me wolde as your brother trete,
And taketh not my frendship in despyt;
And though your sorwes be for thinges grete,
Noot I not why, but out of more respyt,
Myn herte hath for to amende it greet delyt.
And if I may your harmes not redresse,
I am right sory for your hevinesse.

And though ye Troians with us Grekes wrothe
Han many a day be, alwey yet, pardee,
O god of love in sooth we serven bothe.
And, for the love of God, my lady free,
Whom so ye hate, as beth not wroth with me.
For trewely, ther can no wight yow serve,
That half so looth your wraththe wolde
deserve.

And nere it that we been so neigh the tente
Of Calkas, which that seen us bothe may,
I wolde of this yow telle al myn entente;
But this enseled til another day.
Yeve me your hond, I am, and shal ben ay,
God help me so, whyl that my lyf may dure,
Your owene aboven every creature.

Thus seyde I never er now to womman born;
For God myn herte as wisly glade so,
I lovede never womman herebiforn

As paramours, ne never shal no mo.
And, for the love of God, beth not my fo;
Al can I not to yow, my lady dere,
Compleyne aright, for I am yet to lere.

And wondreth not, myn owene lady bright,
Though that I speke of love to you thus blyve;
For I have herd or this of many a wight,
Hath loved thing he never saugh his lyve.
Eek I am not of power for to stryve
Ayens the god of love, but him obeye
I wol alwey, and mercy I yow preye.

Ther been so worthy knightes in this place
And ye so fair, that everich of hem alle
Wol peynen him to stonden in your grace.
But mighte me so fair a grace falle,
That ye me for your servaunt wolde calle,
So lowly ne so trewely you serve
Nil noon of hem, as I shal, til I sterve.

Criseide unto that purpos lyte answerde,
As she that was with sorwe oppressed so
That, in effect, she nought his tales herde,
But here and there, now here a word or two.
Hir thoughte hir sorwful herte brast atwo.
For whan she gan hir fader fer aspye,
Wel neigh doun of hir hors she gan to sye.

And, but you list releve him of his peyne,
Preyeth his beste frend, of his noblesse,
That to som beter estat he may atteyne.
Explicit.

THE COMPLEINT OF CHAUCER TO HIS EMPLY PURSE ❧ ❧

O you, my purse, & to non
other wight
Compleyne I, for ye be my
lady dere!
I am so sory, now that ye be
light;
for certes, but ye make me
hevy chere,
Me were as leef be leyd upon
my bere;
for whiche unto your mercy thus I crye:
Beth hevy ageyn, or elles mot I dye!

Now voucheth sauf this day, or hit be night,
That I of you the blisful soun may here,
Or see your colour lyk the sonne bright,
That of yelownesse hadde never pere.
Ye be my lyf, ye be myn hertes stere,
Quene of comfort and of good companye:
Beth hevy ageyn, or elles mot I dye!

Now purs, that be to me my lyves light,
And saveour, as doun in this worlde here,
Out of this toune help me through your might,
Sin that ye wole nat been my tresorere;
for I am shave as nye as any frere.
But yit I pray unto your curtesye:
Beth hevy ageyn, or elles mot I dye!

Lenvoy de Chaucer.

O CONQUEROUR of Brutes
Albioun!
Which that by lyne and free
eleccioun
Ben verray king, this song to you
I sende;
And ye, that mowen al our harm amende,
Have minde upon my supplicacioun!

MERCILES BEAUTE: A TRIPLE ROUNDEL ❧ ❧

OUR yën two wol slee me
sodenly,
I may the beaute of hem not
sustene,
So woundeth hit throughout
my herte kene.
And but your word wol helen
hastily
My hertes wounde, whyl that
hit is grene,
Your yën two wol slee me sodenly,
I may the beaute of hem not sustene.

Upon my trouthe I sey yow feithfully,
That ye ben of my lyf and deeth the quene;
for with my deeth the trouthe shal be sene.

238

Your yën two wol slee me sodenly,
I may the beaute of hem not sustene,
So woundeth hit throughout my herte kene.

O hath youre beaute fro your herte chaced
Pitee, that me ne availeth not to pleyne;
for Daunger halt your mercy in his cheyne.
Giltles my deeth thus han ye me purchaced;
I sey yow sooth, me nedeth not to feyne;
So hath your beaute fro your herte chaced
Pitee, that me ne availeth not to pleyne.

Allas! that nature hath in yow compassed
So greet beaute, that no man may atteyne
To mercy, though he sterve for the peyne.
So hath your beaute fro your herte chaced
Pitee, that me ne availeth not to pleyne;
for Daunger halt your mercy in his cheyne.

SIN I fro Love escaped am so fat,
I never thenk to ben in his prison lene;
Sin I am free, I counte him not a bene.

He may answere, and seye this or that;
I do no fors, I speke right as I mene.
Sin I fro Love escaped am so fat,
I never thenk to ben in his prison lene.

Love hath my name ystrike out of his sclat,
And he is strike out of my bokes clene
for evermo; ther is non other mene.
Sin I fro Love escaped am so fat,
I never thenk to ben in his prison lene;
Sin I am free, I counte him not a bene.
Explicit.

A COMPLEINT TO HIS LADY ❧ ❧
I.

HE longe night, whan every
creature
Shulde have hir rest in som,
what, as by kinde,
Or elles ne may hir lyf nat
long endure,
Hit falleth most into my
woful minde
How I so fer have broght
myself behinde,
That, sauf the deeth, ther may nothing me lisse,
So desespaired I am from alle blisse.

This same thoght me lasteth til the morwe,
And from the morwe forth til hit be eve;
Ther nedeth me no care for to borwe,
for bothe I have good leyser and good leve;
Ther is no wight that wol me wo bereve
To wepe ynogh, and wailen al my fille;
The sore spark of peyne doth me spille.

II.
The sore spark of peyne doth me spille;
This Love hath eek me set in swich a place
That my desyr he never wol fulfille;
for neither pitee, mercy, neither grace

Can I nat finde; and fro my sorwful herte,
For to be deed, I can hit nat arace.
The more I love, the more she doth me smerte;
Through which I see, withoute remedye,
That from the deeth I may no wyse asterte;
For this day in hir servise shal I dye.

III.

Thus am I slain, with sorwes ful dyverse;
Ful longe agoon I oghte have taken hede.
Now sothly, what she hight I wol reherse;
Hir name is Bountee, set in womanhede,
Sadnesse in youthe, and Beautee prydelees,
And Plesaunce, under governaunce and drede;
Hir surname eek is Faire Rewthelees,
The Wyse, yknit unto Good Aventure,
That, for I love hir, sleeth me giltelees.
Hir love I best, and shal, whyl I may dure,
Bet than myself an hundred thousand deel,
Than al this worldes richesse or creature.
Now hath nat Love me bestowed weel
To love, ther I never shal have part?
Allas! right thus is turned me the wheel,
Thus am I slayn with loves fyry dart.
I can but love hir best, my swete fo;
Love hath me taught no more of his art
But serve alwey, and stinte for no wo.

IV.

Within my trewe careful herte ther is
So moche wo, and eek so litel blis,
That wo is me that ever I was bore;
For al that thing which I desyre I mis,
And al that ever I wolde nat, I wis,
That finde I redy to me evermore;
And of al this I not to whom me pleyne.
For she that mighte me out of this bringe
Ne reccheth nat whether I wepe or singe;
So litel rewthe hath she upon my peyne.

Allas! whan sleping-time is, than I wake,
Whan I shulde daunce, for fere than I quake;
Yow rekketh never wher I flete or sinke;
This hevy lyf I lede for your sake,
Thogh ye therof in no wyse hede take,
For on my wo yow deyneth not to thinke.
My hertes lady, and hool my lyves quene!
For trewly dorste I seye, as that I fele,
Me semeth that your swete herte of stele
Is whetted now ageynes me to kene.

My dere herte, and best beloved fo,
Why lyketh yow to do me al this wo,
What have I doon that greveth yow, or sayd,
But for I serve and love yow and no mo?
And whylst I live, I wol do ever so;
And therfor, swete, ne beth nat evil apayd.
For so good and so fair as that ye be,
Hit were a right gret wonder but ye hadde
Of alle servants, bothe goode and badde;
And leest worthy of alle hem, I am he.

But nevertheles, my righte lady swete,

Thogh that I be unconning and unmete
To serve as I best coude ay your hynesse,
Yit is ther fayner noon, that wolde I hete,
Than I, to do yow ese, or elles bete
Whatso I wiste were to yow distresse.
And hadde I might as good as I have wille,
Than shulde ye fele wher it wer so or noon;
For in this worlde living is ther noon
That fayner wolde your hertes wil fulfille.

For bothe I love, and eek dreed yow so sore,
And algates moot, and have doon yow, ful yore,
That bet loved is noon, ne never shal;
And yit I wolde beseche yow of no more
But leveth wel, and be nat wrooth therfore,
And lat me serve yow forth; lo! this is al.
For I am nat so hardy ne so wood
For to desire that ye shulde love me;
For wel I wot, allas! that may nat be;
I am so litel worthy, and ye so good.

For ye be oon the worthiest on-lyve,
And I the most unlykly for to thryve;
Yit, for al this, now witeth ye right wele,
That ye ne shul me from your service dryve
That I nil ay, with alle my wittes fyve,
Serve yow trewly, what wo so that I fele.
For I am set on yow in swich manere
That, thogh ye never wil upon me rewe,
I moste yow love, and ever been as trewe
As any can or may on-lyve here.

The more that I love yow, goodly free,
The lasse fynde I that ye loven me;
Allas! whan shal that harde wit amende?
Wher is now al your wommanly pitee,
Your gentilesse and your debonairtee,
Wil ye nothing therof upon me spende?
And so hool, swete, as I am youres al,
And so gret wil as I have yow to serve,
Now, certes, and ye lete me thus sterve,
Yit have ye wonne theron but a smal.

For, at my knowing, I do nothing why,
And this I wol beseche yow hertely,
That, ther ever ye finde, whyl ye live,
A trewer servant to yow than am I,
Leveth me thanne, and sleeth me hardely,
And I my deeth to you wol al forgive.
And if ye finde no trewer man than me,
Why will ye suffre than that I thus spille,
And for no maner gilt but my good wille?
As good wer thanne untrewe as trewe to be.

But I, my lyf and deeth, to yow obeye,
And with right buxom herte hoolly I preye,
As is your moste plesure, so doth by me;
Wel lever is me lyken yow and deye
Than for to any thing or thinke or seye
That mighte yow offende in any tyme.
And therfor, swete, rewe on my peynes smerte,

239

outcast thanne thilke provostrie? And, as I have seyd a litel herbiforn, that thilke thing that hath no propre beautee of himself receiveth somtyme prys & shyninge, and somtyme leseth it by the opinioun of usaunces. Now yif that dignitees thanne ne mowen nat maken folk digne of reverence, and yif that dignitees wexen foule of hir wille by the filthe of shrewes, & yif that dignitees lesen hir shyninge by chaunginge of tymes, and yif they wexen foule by estimacioun of poeple: what is it that they han in hemself of beautee that oughte ben desired? as who seyth, non; thanne ne mowen they yeven no beautee of dignitee to non other.

Metre IV.

Quamvis se, Tyrio superbus ostro.

AL be it so that the proude Nero, with alle his wode luxurie, kembde him & aparailede him with faire purpres of Tirie, and with whyte perles, algates yit throf he hateful to alle folk: this is to seyn, that al was he behated of alle folk. Yit this wikked Nero hadde gret lordship, and yaf whylom to the reverents senatours the unworshipful setes of dignitees. Unworshipful setes he clepeth here, for that Nero, that was so wikked, yaf tho dignitees. Whoso wolde thanne resonably wenen, that blisfulnesse were in swiche honours as ben yeven by vicious shrewes?

Prose V.

An vero regna regumque familiaritas.

AT regnes and familiaritees of kinges, may they maken a man to ben mighty? How elles, whan hir blisfulnesse dureth perpetuely? But certes, the olde age of tyme passed, and eek of present tyme now, is ful of ensaumples how that kinges ben chaunged into wrecchednesse out of hir weleful nesse. O! a noble thing and a cleer thing is power, that is nat founden mighty to kepen itself! And yif that power of reaumes be auctour and maker of blisfulnesse, yif thilke power lakketh on any syde, amenuseth it nat thilke blisfulnesse and bringeth in wrecchednesse? But yit, al be it so that the reaumes of mankinde strecchen brode, yit mot ther nede ben moche folk, over whiche that every king ne hath no lordshipe ne comaundement. And certes, upon thilke syde that power faileth, which that maketh folk blisful, right on that same

348

syde noun-power entreth undernethe, that maketh hem wrecches; in this manere thanne moten kinges han more porcioun of wrecchednesse than of welefulnesse. A tyraunt, that was king of Sisile, that hadde assayed the peril of his estat, shewede by similitude the dredes of reaumes by gastnesse of a swerd that heng over the heved of his familier. What thing is thanne this power, that may nat don awey the bytinges of bisinesse, ne eschewe the prikkes of drede? And certes, yit wolden they liven in sikernesse, but they may nat; and yit they glorifye hem in hir power. Holdest thou thanne that thilke man be mighty, that thou seest that he wolde don that he may nat don? And holdest thou thanne him a mighty man, that hath envirownede his sydes with men of armes or serjaunts, & dredeth more hem that he maketh agast than they dreden him, and that is put in the handes of his servaunts for he sholde seme mighty? But of familieres or servaunts of kinges what sholde I telle thee anything, sin that I myself have shewed thee that reaumes hemself ben ful of gret feblesse? The whiche familieres, certes, the ryal power of kinges, in hool estat and in estat abated, ful ofte throweth adown. Nero constreynede Senek, his familier and his mayster, to chesen on what deeth he wolde deyen. Antonius comaundede that knightes slowen with hir swerdes Papinian his familier, which Papinian hadde ben longe tyme ful mighty amonges hem of the court. And yit, certes, they wolden bothe han renounced hir power; of whiche two Senek enforcede him to yeven to Nero his richesses, & also to han gon into solitarie exil. But whan the grete weighte, that is to seyn, of lordes power or of fortune, draweth hem that shullen falle, neither of hem ne mighte do that he wolde. What thing is thanne thilke power, that though men han it, yit they ben agast; and whanne thou woldest han it, thou nart nat siker; & yif thou woldest forleten it, thou mayst nat eschuen it? But whether swiche men ben frendes at nede, as ben conseyled by fortune and nat by vertu? Certes, swiche folk as weleful fortune maketh freendes, contrarious fortune maketh hem enemys. And what pestilence is more mighty for to anoye a wight than a familier enemy?

Metre V.

Qui se volet esse potentem.

HOSO wol be mighty, he mot daunten his cruel corage, ne putte nat his nekke, overcomen, under the foule reynes of lecherye. For albeit so that thy lordshipe strecche so fer, that the contree of Inde quaketh at thy comaundements or at thy lawes, and that the last ile in the see, that hight Tyle, be thral to thee, yit, yif thou mayst nat putten awey thy foule derke desyrs, & dryven out fro thee wrecched complaintes, certes, it nis no power that thou hast.

Prose VI.
Gloria vero quam fallax saepe.

UT glorie, how deceivable and how foul is it ofte! For which thing nat unskilfully a tragedien, that is to seyn, a maker of ditees that highten tragedies, cryde & seide: O glorie, glorie, quod he, thou art nothing elles to thousandes of folkes but a greet sweller of eres! For manye han had ful greet renoun by the false opinioun of the poeple, and what thing may ben thought fouler than swiche preysinge? For thilke folk that ben preysed falsly, they moten nedes han shame of hir preysinges. And yif that folk han geten hem thonk or preysinge by hir desertes, what thing hath thilke prys eched or encresed to the conscience of wyse folk, that mesuren hir good, nat by the rumour of the poeple, but by the soothfastnesse of conscience? And yif it seme a fair thing, a man to han encresed and spred his name, than folweth it that it is demed to ben a foul thing, yif it ne be ysprad and encresed. But, as I seyde a litel herbiforn that, sin ther mot nedes ben many folk, to whiche folk the renoun of a man ne may nat comen, it befalleth that he, that thou wenest be glorious and renomed, semeth in the nexte partie of the erthes to ben withoute glorie and withoute renoun.

ND certes, amonges thise thinges I ne trowe nat that the prys & grace of the poeple nis neither worthy to ben remembred, ne cometh of wyse jugement, ne is ferme perdurably. But now, of this name of gentilesse, what man is it that ne may wel seen how veyn & how flitinge a thing it is? For yif the name of gentilesse be referred to renoun & cleernesse of linage, thanne is gentil name but a foreine thing, that is to seyn, to hem that glorifyen hem of hir linage. For it semeth that gentilesse be a maner preysinge that comth of the deserte of ancestres. And yif preysinge maketh gentilesse, thanne moten they nedes be gentil that ben preysed. For which thing it folweth, that yif thou ne have no gentilesse of thyself, that is to seyn, preyse that comth of thy deserte,

foreine gentilesse ne maketh thee nat gentil. But certes, yif ther be any good in gentilesse, I trowe it be alonly this, that it semeth as that a maner necessitee be imposed to gentil men, for that they ne sholden nat outrayen or forliven fro the virtues of hir noble kinrede.

Metre VI.
Omne hominum genus in terris.

L the linage of men that ben in erthe ben of semblable birthe. On allone is fader of thinges. On allone ministreth alle thinges. He yaf to the sonne hise bemes; he yaf to the mone hir hornes. He yaf the men to the erthe; he yaf the sterres to the hevene. He encloseth with membres the soules that comen fro his hye sete. Thanne comen alle mortal folk of noble sede; why noisen ye or bosten of youre eldres? For yif thou loke your biginninge, and God your auctor & your maker, thanne nis ther no forlived wight, but yif he norisshe his corage unto vyces, and forlete his propre burthe.

Prose VII.
Quid autem de corporis voluptatibus.

UT what shal I seye of delices of body, of whiche delices the desiringes ben ful of anguissh, & the fulfillinges of hem ben ful of penaunce? How greet syknesse and how grete sorwes unsufferable, right as a maner fruit of wikkednesse, ben thilke delices wont to bringen to the bodies of folk that usen hem! Of whiche delices I not what joye may ben had of hir moevinge. But this wot I wel, that whosoever wole remembren him of hise luxures, he shal wel understonde that the issues of delices ben sorwful & sorye. And yif thilke delices mowen maken folk blisful, than by the same cause moten thise bestes ben cleped blisful; of whiche bestes al the entencioun hasteth to fulfille hir bodily jolitee. And the gladnesse of wyf and children were an honest thing, but it hath ben seyd that it is over muchel ayeins kinde, that children han ben founden tormentours to hir fadres, I not how manye: of whiche children how bytinge is every condicioun, it nedeth nat to tellen it thee, that hast or this tyme assayed it, and art yit now anguissous. In this approve I the sentence of my disciple Euripidis, that seyde, that He that hath no children is weleful by infortune.

349

As I shal telle yow echoon.

FIRST saw I the destruccioun
Of Troye, through the Greek
Sinoun,
That with his false forsweringe,
And his chere and his lesinge
Made the hors broght into Troye,
Thorgh which Troyens loste al hir joye.
And after this was grave, allas!
How Ilioun assailed was
And wonne, and king Priam yslayn,
And Polites his sone, certayn,
Dispitously, of dan Pirrus.

AND next that saw I how Venus,
Whan that she saw the castel brende,
Doun fro the hevene gan descende,
And bad hir sone Eneas flee;
And how he fledde, and how that he
Escaped was from al the pres,
And took his fader, Anchises,
And bar him on his bakke away,
Cryinge, Allas, and welaway!
The whiche Anchises in his honde
Bar the goddes of the londe,
Thilke that unbrende were.

AND I saw next, in alle this fere,
How Creusa, daun Eneas wyf,
Which that he lovede as his lyf,
And hir yonge son Julo,
And eek Ascanius also,
Fledden eek with drery chere,
That hit was pitee for to here;
And in a forest, as they wente,
At a turninge of a wente,
How Creusa was ylost, allas!
That deed, but noot I how, she was;
How he hir soughte, and how hir gost
Bad him to flee the Grekes ost,
And seyde, he moste unto Itaile,
As was his destinee, sauns faille;
That hit was pitee for to here,
Whan hir spirit gan appere,
The wordes that she to him seyde,
And for to kepe hir sone him preyde.
Ther saw I graven eek how he,
His fader eek, and his meynee,
With his shippes gan to sayle
Toward the contree of Itaile,
As streight as that they mighte go.

THER saw I thee, cruel Juno,
That art daun Jupiteres wyf,
That hast yhated, al thy lyf,
Al the Troyanisshe blood,
Renne and crye, as thou were wood,
On Eolus, the god of windes,
To blowen out, of alle kindes,
So loude, that he shulde drenche
Lord and lady, grome and wenche
Of al the Troyan nacioun,
Withoute any savacioun.

THER saw I swich tempeste aryse,
That every herte mighte agryse,
To see hit peynted on the walle.

450

THER saw I graven eek withalle,
Venus, how ye, my lady dere,
Wepinge with ful woful chere,
Prayen Jupiter an hye
To save and kepe that navye
Of the Troyan Eneas,
Sith that he hir sone was.

THER saw I Joves Venus kisse,
And graunted of the tempest lisse.
Ther saw I how the tempest stente,
And how with alle pyne he wente,
And prevely took arrivage
In the contree of Cartage;
And on the morwe, how that he
And a knight, hight Achatee,
Metten with Venus that day,
Goinge in a queynt array,
As she had ben an hunteresse,
With wind blowinge upon hir tresse;
How Eneas gan him to pleyne,
Whan that he knew hir, of his peyne;
And how his shippes dreynte were,
Or elles lost, he niste where;
How she gan him comforte tho,
And bad him to Cartage go,
And ther he shuldë his folk finde,
That in the see were left behinde.

AND, shortly of this thing to pace,
She made Eneas so in grace
Of Dido, quene of that contree,
That, shortly for to tellen, she
Becam his love, and leet him do
That that wedding longeth to.
What shulde I speke more queynte,
Or peyne me my wordes peynte,
To speke of love? hit wol not be;
I can not of that facultee.
And eek to telle the manere
How they aqueynteden in fere,
Hit were a long proces to telle,
And over long for yow to dwelle.

THER saw I grave, how Eneas
Tolde Dido every cas,
That him was tid upon the see.

AND after grave was, how she
Made of him, shortly, at oo word,
Hir lyf, hir love, hir lust, hir lord;
And dide him al the reverence,
And leyde on him al the dispence,
That any woman mighte do,
Weninge hit had al be so,
As he hir swoor; and herby demed
That he was good, for he swich semed.
Allas! what harm doth apparence,
Whan hit is fals in existence!
For he to hir a traitour was;
Wherfor she slow hirself, allas!

LO, how a woman doth amis,
To love him that unknowen is!
For, by Crist, lo! thus hit fareth;
Hit is not al gold, that glareth.
For, also brouke I wel myn heed,
Ther may be under goodliheed

Kevered many a shrewed vyce;
Therfor be no wight so nyce,
To take a love only for chere,
For speche, or for frendly manere;
For this shal every woman finde
That som man, of his pure kinde,
Wol shewen outward the faireste,
Til he have caught that what him leste;
And thanne wol he causes finde,
And swere how that she is unkinde,
Or fals, or prevy, or double was.
Al this seye I by Eneas
And Dido, and hir nyce lest,
That lovede al to sone a gest;
Therfor I wol seye a proverbe,
That He that fully knoweth therbe
May saufly leye hit to his yë
Withoute dreed, this is no lye.

BUT let us speke of Eneas,
How he betrayed hir, allas!
And lefte hir ful unkindely.
So whan she saw al utterly,
That he wolde hir of trouthe
faile,
And wende fro hir to Itaile,
She gan to wringe hir hondes two.

ALLAS! quod she, what me is wo!
Allas! is every man thus trewe,
That every yere wolde have a newe,
If hit so longe tyme dure,
Or elles three, peraventure?
As thus: of oon he wolde have fame
In magnifying of his name;
Another for frendship, seith he;
And yet ther shal the thridde be,
That shal be taken for delyt,
Lo, or for singular profyt.

IN swiche wordes gan to pleyne
Dido of grete peyne,
As me mette redely;
Non other auctour alegge I.
Allas! quod she, my swete herte,
Have pitee on my sorwes smerte,
And slee me not! go noght away!
O woful Dido, wel away!
Quod she to hirselve tho.
O Eneas! what wil ye do?
O, that your love, ne your bonde,
That ye han sworn with your right honde,
Ne my cruel deeth, quod she,
May holde yow still heer with me!
O, haveth of my deeth pitee!
Ywis, my dere herte, ye
Knowen ful wel that never yit,
As ferforth as I hadde wit,
Agilte I yow in thoght ne deed.
O, have ye men swich goodliheed
In speche, and never a deel of trouthe?
Allas, that ever hadde routhe
Any woman on any man!
Now see I wel, and telle can,
We wrecched wimmen conne non art;
For certeyn, for the more part,
g g 2

Thus we be served everichone.
How sore that ye men conne grone,
Anoon, as we have yow receyved,
Certeinly we ben deceyved;
For, though your love laste a sesoun,
Wayte upon the conclusioun,
And eek how that ye determynen,
And for the more part diffynen.

O, WELAWEY that I was born!
For through yow is my name lorn,
And alle myn actes red and songe
Over al this lond, on every tonge.
O wikke fame! for ther nis
Nothing so swift, lo, as she is!
O, sooth is, every thing is wist,
Though hit be kevered with the mist.
Eek, thogh I mighte duren ever,
That I have doon, rekever I never,
That I ne shal be seyd, allas,
Yshamed be through Eneas,
And that I shal thus juged be:
Lo, right as she hath doon, now she
Wol do eftsones, hardily,
Thus seyth the peple prevely.

BUT that is doon, nis not to done;
Al hir compleynt ne al hir mone,
Certeyn, availeth hir not a stre.

AND whan she wiste sothly he
Was forth unto his shippes goon,
She in hir chambre wente anoon,
And called on hir suster Anne,
And gan hir to compleyne thanne;
And seyde, that she cause was
That she first lovede Eneas,
And thus counseilled hir therto.
But what! when this was seyd and do,
She roof hirselve to the herte,
And deyde through the wounde smerte.
But al the maner how she deyde,
And al the wordes that she seyde,
Whoso to knowe hit hath purpos,
Reed Virgile in Eneidos
Or the Epistle of Ovyde,
What that she wroot or that she dyde;
And nere hit to long to endyte,
By God, I woldë hit here wryte.

BUT, welaway! the harm, the routhe,
That hath betid for swich untrouthe,
As men may ofte in bokes rede,
And al day seen hit yet in dede,
That for to thenken hit, a tene is.

LO, Demophon, duk of Athenis,
How he forswor him ful falsly,
And trayed Phillis wikkedly,
That kinges doghter was of Trace,
And falsly gan his terme pace;
And when she wiste that he was
fals,
She heng hirself right by the hals,
For he had do hir swich untrouthe;
Lo! was not this a wo and routhe?
EEK lo! how fals and reccheles
Was to Briseida Achilles,

451

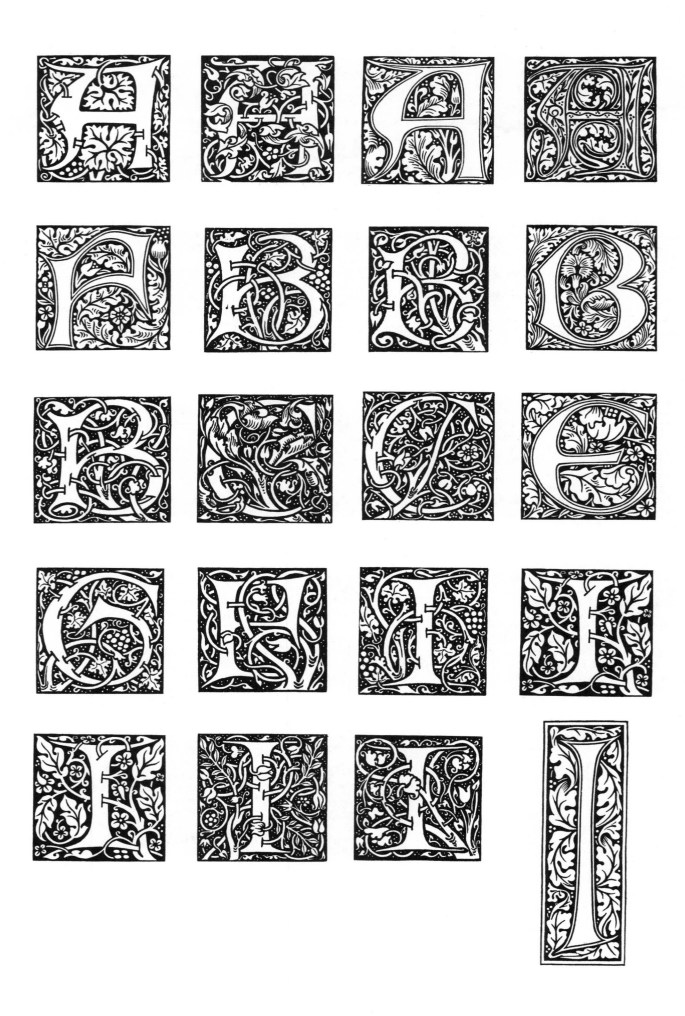

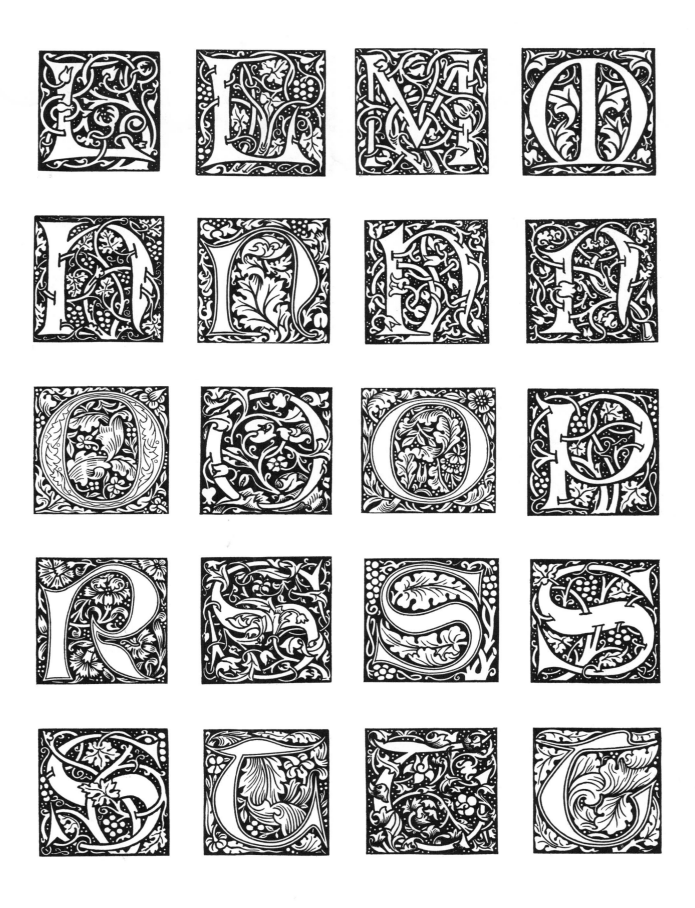

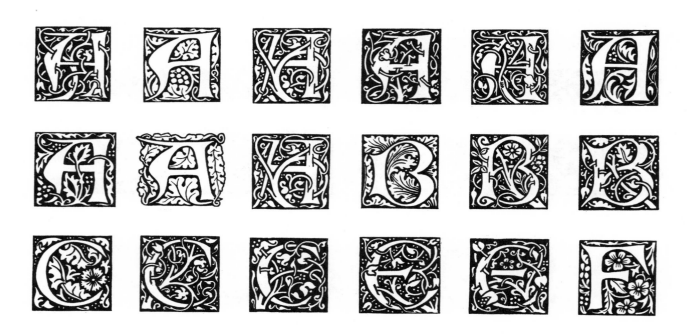